COSTUME DESIGN
GRAPHICS

A WORKBOOK IN
FIGURE DRAWING
AND CLOTHING TECHNIQUES

D1452170

COSTUME DESIGN GRAPHICS

A WORKBOOK IN
FIGURE DRAWING
AND CLOTHING TECHNIQUES

RORY SCANLON

COSTUME & FASHION PRESS
NEW YORK • HOLLYWOOD
an imprint of
Quite Specific Media Group Ltd.

Production Editor: Judith Durant
Book Design and Production: Ascienzo Design
Cover Photograph: Joe Coca

Costume & Fashion Press
an imprint of
Quite Specific Media Group Ltd.
7373 Pyramid Place
Hollywood, CA 90046

Business Office:
212.725.5377 voice • 212.725.8506 fax
email:info@quitespecificmedia.com
http://www.quitespecificmedia.com

Other Quite Specific Media Group Ltd. Imprints:
Drama Publishers
By Design Press
EntertainmentPro
Jade Rabbit

Library of Congress Cataloging in Publication Data
Scanlon, Rory, 1954–
    Costume design graphics : a workbook in figure drawing and clothing techniques / Rory Scanlon.
      p.   cm.
    Includes index.
    ISBN 0-89676-236-X (alk. paper)
    1. Fashion drawing. 2. Costume design. 1. Title.

TT509 .S27 2000
741.6'72—dc21   00-064339

To my wife; my best critic
and my best friend.

As an educator and professional designer, I have long sensed the need for a book on developing graphic techniques for costume designers. The approaches I've used are a mixture of techniques I have picked up from colleagues or developed while solving my own rendering problems.

This book in no way professes to hold the "gospel of costume graphics," but contains approaches and ideas for both beginners and professionals, providing exercises for you, the reader, to use and experiment with. Each section depends on the one before to develop its process, so even if you feel confident in one or more areas you should complete each section.

I have found that my graphic skills as a costume designer need to be continually honed, even as I begin to settle on techniques that seem to work best for me; part of every artist's skill is to adapt any technique into his or her own "style." The exercises in this book, then, should not become your ultimate technique but instead another door to the continual progression you should experience as you better learn to communicate on that blank piece of paper.

This book is dedicated to all designers. And though we share the common challenge of expressing ourselves in a rendering, the graphic work we do is only a small part of our job. The application of what we've drawn to the costumes worn on stage makes us who we really are. The education of costume designers often emphasizes the drawing itself because there isn't time for each class project to be realized in the shop. We need to emphasize that a rendering is created to service the stage; it is not a piece of art in itself, but a blueprint for the final product. The process of expressing your ideas is in reality the technique of "capturing" your ideas on paper, much as the playwright captures a skeletal form of a play on the pages of a script. As long as you can see through your work to the finished costume, you'll maintain the proper perspective. Lines and colors will come more easily, and attention will focus on the three-dimensional product created beneath the hands of the stitchers. But just as a pianist must first master the keyboard and learn to read music well enough that it becomes second nature, you must first become confident enough in your graphic abilities if the final product is to retain its proper emphasis.

I believe there's a designer in each of us, and education is not meant to "make" us designers nor even to teach us how to draw. What we learn should, instead, help us understand why we feel as we do and how to communicate that to an audience. I encourage you to trust your instincts in the initial design—to sketch first from your intuitive feelings about the script without being weighed down with "design rules." Later, you can apply design principles to critique and improve what you've created. This workbook is meant to help in that "why" process, especially in "how" to communicate to the director and shop, and through them to the audience.

I would appreciate your feedback, and encourage you to share your views with others as well. We should all be more open in our graphic art—with our students, with our colleagues, and especially with ourselves.

CONTENTS

Undoubtedly, you have glanced through this book and are aware that it is different in that it is visual. First of all, this is a workbook. It is presented in a step-by-step manner to encourage you to draw as you go. Nothing teaches you graphic techniques faster than your own mistakes... and successes! And *do not* draw small, one inch figures! Work with ten to twelve inch forms. After all, if you're going to make mistakes, make them big! You will not learn from "fudging" your errors in miniature. If you want to solve your problems, draw large and deal with them. That's why you're reading this book in the first place, isn't it?

I encourage you to question. Question everything in this book and try other ways to produce your image. If you only want to copy, you'll be frustrated. You can never successfully produce someone else's work. And why would you want to? Your style is unique. Your goal should be to perfect *that* technique by trying *other* techniques. My process is a product of many other peoples' techniques. It would be difficult to determine the source of any specific element.

Much of your frustration at this point is due to the fact that you find others who draw "better" than you. Stop that way of thinking and simply realize that they draw "differently" from you, that's all. And that's the way it's supposed to be!

As a designer, you will need to develop your *own* techniques. These techniques will include the need to (1) produce quick sketches with a minimum of effort, (2) create finished renderings with a minimum of effort, and (3) produce working drawings with a minimum of effort. In other words, *a minimum of effort* is the key to keeping ahead of your field. Hours and hours at the drawing table will only produce drawings and that is not the goal. Finished costumes on stage is the goal. Don't spend all your time producing wall hangings. Remember that the drawings and renderings you create are only one step toward a finished costume. The rendering communicates construction information to the shop, character interpretation to the director, coloring and texture choices to the lighting designer, form and flow possibilities to the scenic designer, and shape and weight conditions to the actor. It is a working form for developing your ideas. That's a lot of information on one piece of paper! That may be why you're afraid of it, but now it's time to eliminate the fear and begin.

And herein is the purpose of the book: not *reading* about costume design, but *designing costumes!* Chapters are set up so that the reading is a preface to the drawing. Lay down the pencil from time to time and read for ideas and recommendations. After all, I took the time to write them! But spend most of your time with the drawing segments. Use a sheet of drawing paper, use the table top— but *draw!* This is the only way you will achieve improvement and success in graphic communication.

This book is meant to remind you what your "tools" are as a costume designer, help you master their use, and encourage you to continue to find new ways to employ them. We should all be "continuing students" in art, research, and construction. Never stop learning. Never stop observing. To do so would be to prevent yourself from being the designer you should be.

So, get out a pencil and let's start *designing.*

The true talent of the artist is not necessarily the ability to draw, but rather the ability to see objects differently. Instead of drawing a tree, the artist approaches his work by rendering line, form, texture, color and value in order for a tree to emerge. These are known as the elements of design and are nothing more than the "tools" an artist uses to communicate what he sees onto a piece of paper. The artist learns to draw what he actually sees, and not what he thinks he sees.

In her fascinating book *Drawing On the Right Side of the Brain,* Betty Edwards deals with the symbolic labeling system of the human mind. Sometime in our early years we recorded "symbols" for objects around us and, generally, these symbols were as simple as our artistic ability was at the time we recorded them. These rudimentary symbols are what we pull from our mind as we draw trees, flowers, houses, and human bodies. Rather than drawing what we have before us, the majority of us will reproduce these mental "symbols," perhaps adapting them somewhat in angle or size to agree with the object we think we're drawing.

Ms. Edwards' book deals principally with studio art and we must realize the full impact of this theory on the designer. While the studio artist works from real objects, we, as designers, are dealing heavily with mental images. If, indeed, our work is mainly cerebral, it's easy to see how the "symbols" of our past can limit our drawing abilities. Obviously, it is extremely important to "retrain" our minds by replacing the childhood symbols with symbols that are more applicable to our art form. This demands hours of drawing, an area in which the student and professional alike must constantly be actively engaged. Nothing can compensate for a good figure drawing class, but the class itself will not fulfill the need until the student learns to see differently. It is important to begin registering symbols in the mind for all parts of the human body, in all their variations of angle and position...simple, right?

One practice used effectively by studio artists is tracing or copying master artists' work. This can also be quite effective for the graphic artist. Each student should fill a tracing pad with hands, faces, feet and full bodies from a number of sources including commercial pattern books, fashion magazines, and newspaper ads—anywhere graphic human forms can be found. We refer to this pad of images as a "Body Morgue" and it is quite useful to the designer during the drawing stages. But more valuable to the artist are the "mental images" that have now been transferred in the process. The mind has an incredible ability to remember what the hand has experienced, and once the artist has traced enough, he can usually reproduce without visual reference. Even if the initial reproductive process is slow, the student will have a pad of tracings to use as reference or direct transfer until he or she feels more confident in his or her own ability.

Before moving on to actual drawing techniques, permit me to mention again the value of Betty Edwards' book and her step-by-step process of learning to "see again." Her fascinating exercises are useful classroom material for helping students realize they can, indeed, draw. It also aids them in discovering that what has prevented them from doing so has been the limited "symbol" file upon which they have relied. If the simple fear of "blank paper" looms before you, pick up Ms. Edwards' book and work through the exercises *before* you begin the exercises in this book. And even if you feel you've mastered "pencil-phobia," take a look at her book anyway. After all, it couldn't hurt.

APPROACHES TO RENDERING THE HUMAN FIGURE

The most difficult object for many people to draw is the human form. Its complexity of angle, shape and ever-changing gesture eludes even the most talented artist. The costume designer must understand the figure enough to be able to use it as a canvas for his or her creations. Therefore, an introduction to human structure, as well as intrinsic capabilities of physical expression, will enhance the designer's confidence and rendering techniques.

The artist needs to work with some constant measurement as he sketches, something by which to compare the proportion of each piece in his picture. As we approach drawing the human figure, we will use the human head as that constant measuring device and learn to proportion the figure in *Heads*.

The average human body is 7^1/$_2$ Heads tall as shown in this illustration. Notice the points of reference determined by each Head. Partial Heads are shown with dotted lines.

Here is a breakdown of the human form by Heads, beginning at the top.

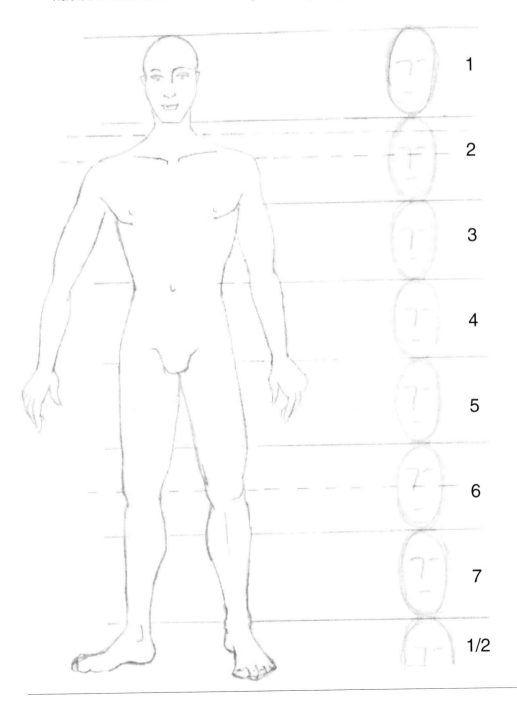

1: The head itself

1^1/$_4$: Bottom of neck

1^1/$_2$: Shoulder point

2: Bust point

3: Waist

4: Crotch

5^1/$_2$: Knee

7: Ankle

7 ^{1}/$_2$: Bottom of foot (ground)

Body widths can also be determined by Heads. This illustration shows the male and female bodies in comparison of widths. Please note that the Head measurement is turned sideways for these calibrations.

Here is a breakdown by Heads for essential widths.

Male shoulders: 2 Heads
Female shoulders: 1^1/$_2$ Heads

Male chest: 1^1/$_2$ Heads
Female chest: 1^1/$_4$ Heads

Male waist: 1^1/$_4$ Heads
Female waist: 1 Head

Male hips: 1^1/$_2$ Heads
Female hips: 1^1/$_2$ Heads

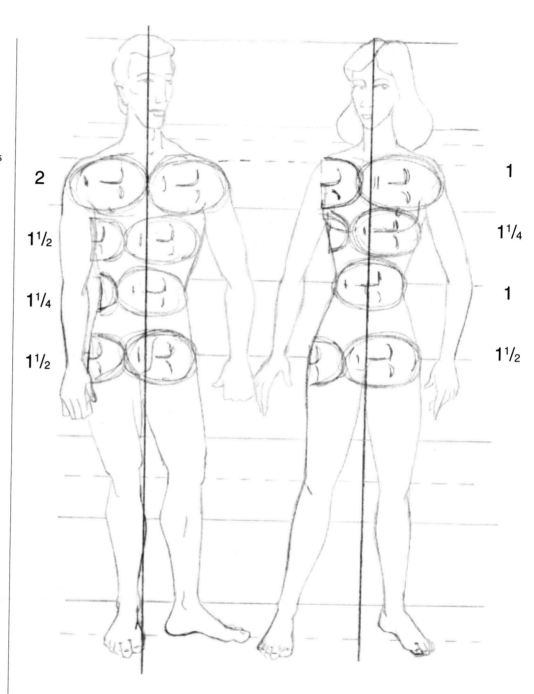

Note especially that both male and female hips are the same in Head widths, but the difference in proportion to the rest of the body creates the masculine and feminine physique.

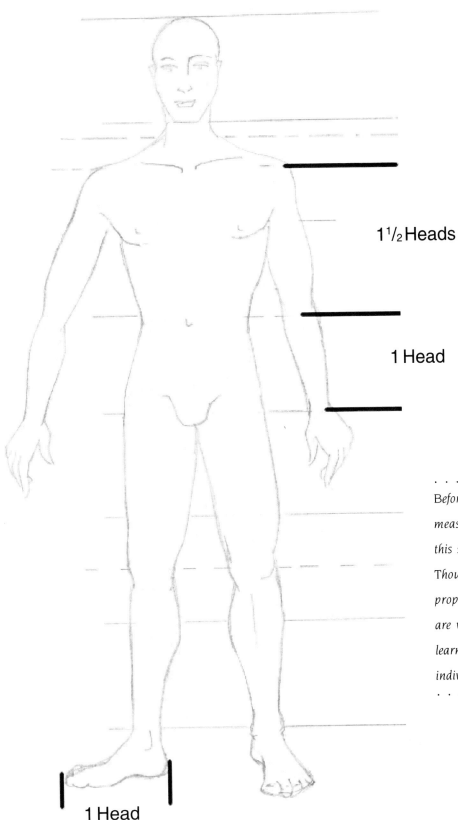

1½ Heads

1 Head

1 Head

OTHER PROPORTIONS:
For quick reference, note the following proportional ratios and compare them with the illustration–

Upper arm: same as shoulder point to waist, or 1½ Heads

Lower arm: same as "waist" to crotch, or one Head

Foot length: same as lower arm, or about one Head

Before we approach drawing a figure using this measurement system, we must mention that this system produces a "generic" human form. Though each individual varies uniquely is some proportions, generally speaking, most people are very close to these measurements. We will learn later how to adapt the system for different individual body types.

APPLYING THE PROPORTIONS: THE GLASS TECHNIQUE

With a working knowledge of human proportions, let us use these dimensions to create a male body. Find a pencil and paper and work along with each step. Don't copy, use the steps as an example and work on your own figure. You may find it easier to read through the process first and then go back step by step with your own drawing. Whichever way you wish to proceed...*draw!*

As a basic philosophy, think of the figure you draw as though it were made of glass. Don't worry about what part of the body is covered by other parts, draw everything to begin with. This is what we refer to as the "Glass Technique." It will allow us to see all parts of the body at all times. We will later erase the "hidden" lines to complete the figure for a more realistic, two-dimensional view.

1. Begin by drawing an oval to represent the placement of the head somewhere toward the top of your paper. Using your fingers, a ruler, or some other measuring device, repeat that Head measurement down the page, marking off 6$\frac{1}{2}$ additional Heads.

1

2

3

4

5

6

7

1/2

2. **Divide Head 2 and Head 5 in half by drawing dotted lines to locate the shoulder and knee points respectively.**

3. **Divide the top half of Head 2 one more time with a dotted line to locate the bottom of the neck.**

. . . .

Knowing the full size of the body at this point allows you to adjust the size or placement to better use your paper space. A figure from ten to twelve inches tall is ideal. This would suggest the use of drawing paper about fourteen inches in length.

. . . .

4. **Draw a line down from the center of the oval to locate the Center Front line of the body. This line is important for measuring "widths" and will also be helpful later on in clothing the figure.**

5. **Apply two Heads evenly centered on the Center Front line to find the shoulder points out along the dotted shoulder mark. Remember, turn the Heads sideways for all of these measurements.**

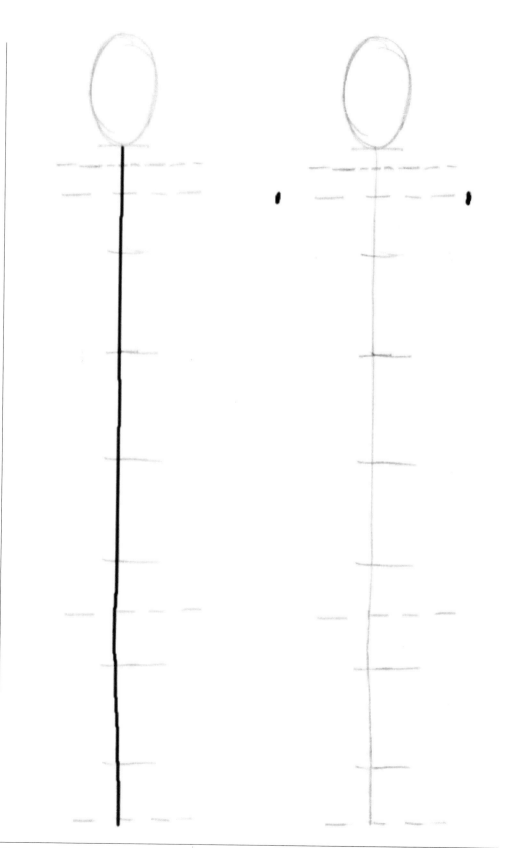

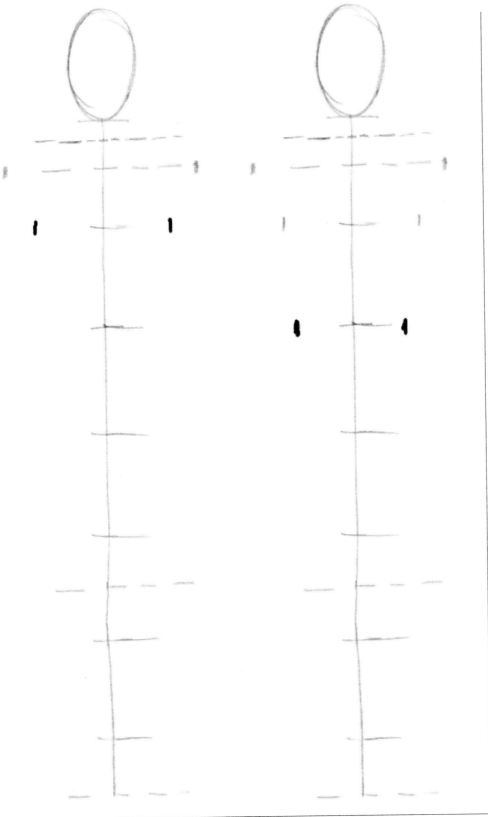

6. Apply 1$\frac{1}{2}$ Heads evenly centered on the Center Front line to find the sides of the chest at the second Head mark.

7. Apply 1$\frac{1}{4}$ Heads evenly centered on the Center Front line to find the sides of the waist at the third Head mark.

8. Apply 1¹/₂ Heads (yes, the same as the "chest") evenly centered on the Center Front line to find the sides of the hips at the fourth Head mark.

9. Draw the neck down from the head oval to the quarter mark of Head 2.

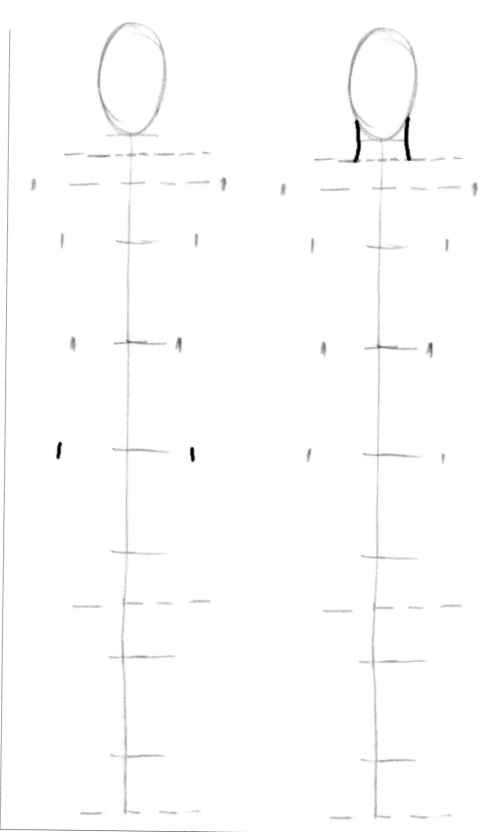

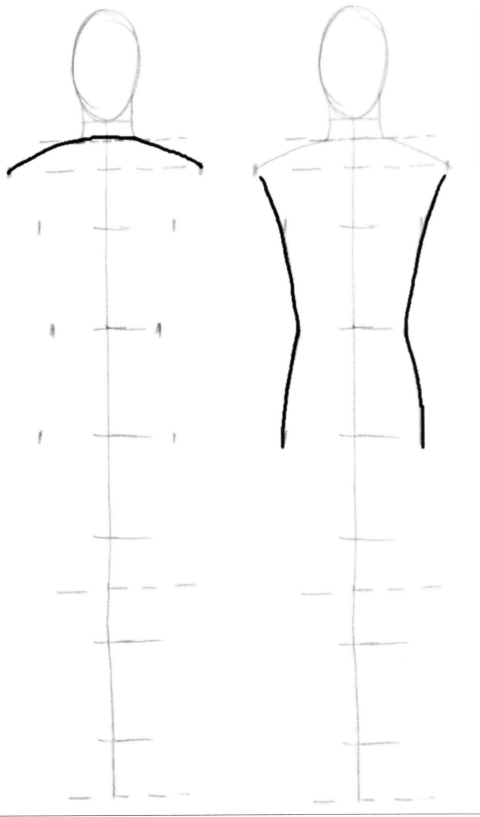

10. Now draw the shoulder curve in from shoulder point to shoulder point, connecting it with the base of the neck.

11. A dot-to-dot connection of existing marks at this point will give you a rough torso and hip line.

12. Sketch in the *shoulder joints* **at this point. They are roughly one-half to three-quarters Head in size. Note that each joint** *adds* **dimension to the overall shoulder width. It extends somewhat from the shoulder point, both up and out, broadening the shoulders a bit from the initial two Heads width.**

13. Sketch in the *hip joints* **next. These joints run diagonally along a "panty line," from the high hip at an angle down to the center of the crotch mark. We'll refer to these joints as the "butterfly" since that's what they look like when sketched in.**

With the joints placed, we can now add appendages. The legs are important at this point to support and balance the figure.

We will use the Center Front line as a Plummet Line to determine the weight distribution of the figure. A Plummet Line is a vertical gravity line, used particularly for keeping things at a 90° angle from their foundation. Note that the general rule of balance for the figures we draw is this: *The Plummet Line must stay* within *the inside ankles of the two legs for the body to be supported.* To stand on one foot, the body must be positioned so that the Plummet Line is directly over the inside ankle of the supporting foot.

You may wish to stand in front of a mirror and try some repositioning of your Plummet Line to see how your legs support your body. Don't be embarrassed, nobody is watching!

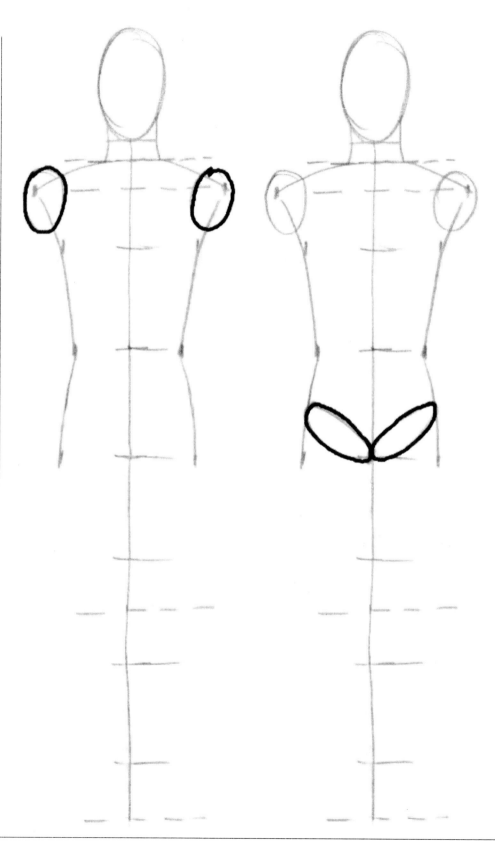

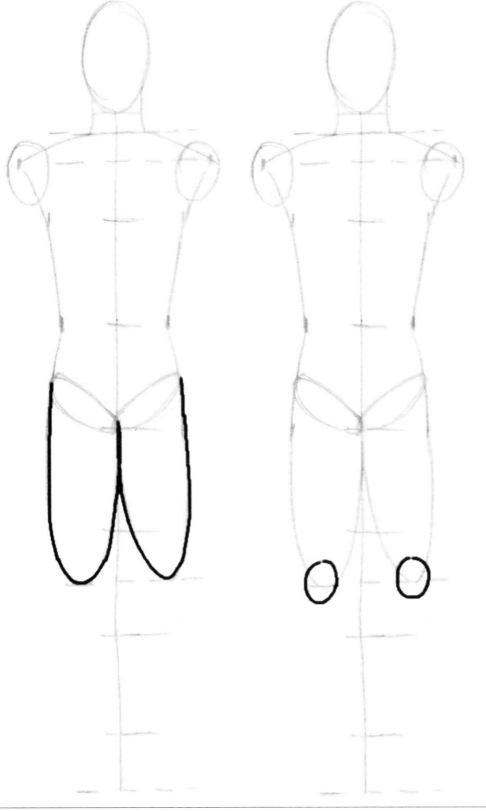

Note that it *is* possible to push the Plummet Line *past* an inside ankle. To do so, however, you have to thrust the other leg in the opposite direction to create "ballast." Sometimes the arms or the upper body are also used to counter the effects of gravity. Try a few positions in the mirror and see how the Plummet Line concept explains how your body and legs move to support one another.

14. **Now, let us return to our figure. Keep in mind that we must position the legs to keep the Plummet Line *within* the inside ankles. Draw the thighs with long ovals that encompass the hip joint at the top and extend down to the dotted line at 5 1/2 Heads. Make sure that the top of the oval encloses the *entire* hip joint.**

15. **Sketch in a knee joint, centered on the dotted line and encompassing part of the thigh oval. This joint is roughly one-half Head in size.**

16. From the center of the knee joint, sketch the lower leg oval, extending down to the seventh Head mark.

17. The feet can be sketched into the remaining one-half Head area. Keep them simple at this point; we can detail the feet later.

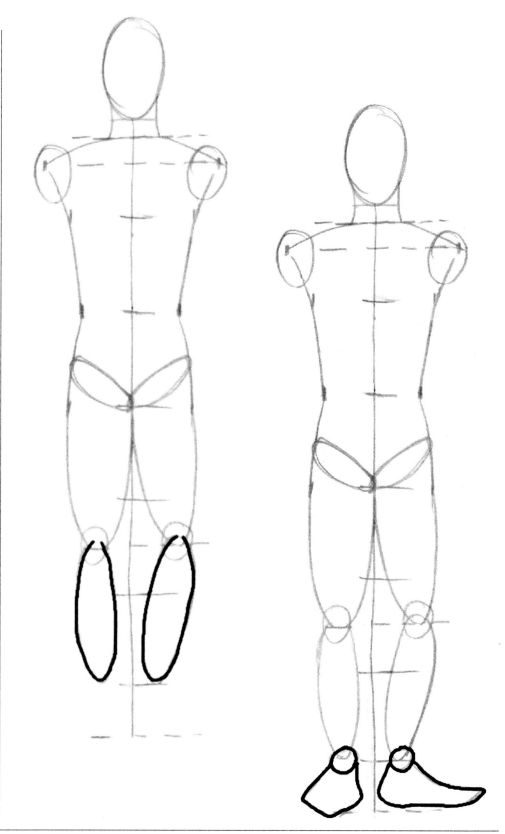

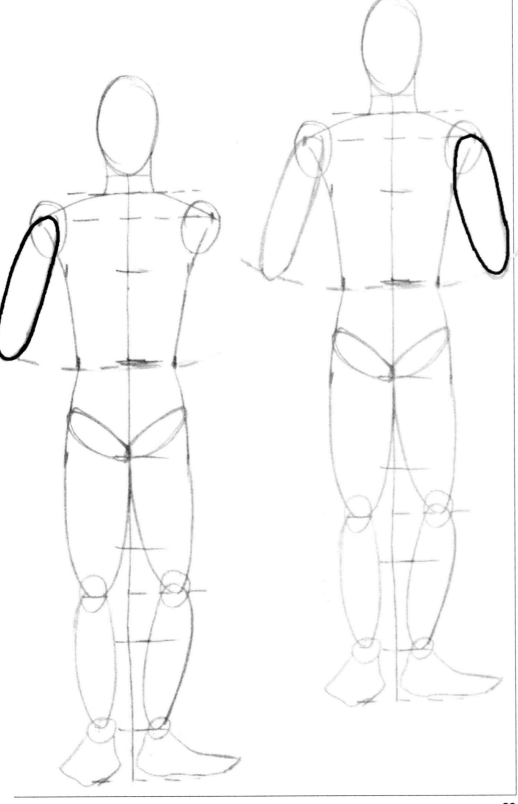

Now let us sketch in the upper arm. Its length is $1\frac{1}{2}$ Heads, or, conveniently, the distance from the shoulder point to the waist.

18. **The sketch here shows that the "elbow length" of the arm travels within an arc drawn through the waist. Therefore, we can position the arm by taking a $1\frac{1}{2}$ Head measurement from the shoulder point down to the waist using our thumb and forefinger, or any other measuring device. Swing the "length" out from the shoulder point and mark the extension. Draw in an oval from the center of the shoulder joint out to the $1\frac{1}{2}$ Head mark we just made. Draw the other upper arm in the same manner.**

19. An elbow joint can be sketched at this point, if we wish, but the elbow joint doesn't tend to add much dimension to the arm. It is mainly incorporated into the upper and lower arm shapes.

The lower arm is one Head long, or, conveniently, the distance from the waist to the crotch. *(Yes, the elbow is positioned directly at the waist, and the wrist is directly at the crotch.)* Remember, these are "ideal" body proportions and though each of us differs somewhat, we generally follow the rules.

Take a one-Head measurement and apply it out from the elbow joint. Sketch the lower arms. *Be true to the limitations of the human elbow joint! It only has about an 80° arc of movement.*

20. The hands can be sketched in very simply for now. No need for detailing; we are just learning proportions. The hand is roughly three-quarters of a Head, or the length of the face, but we will study these proportions more specifically in just a moment.

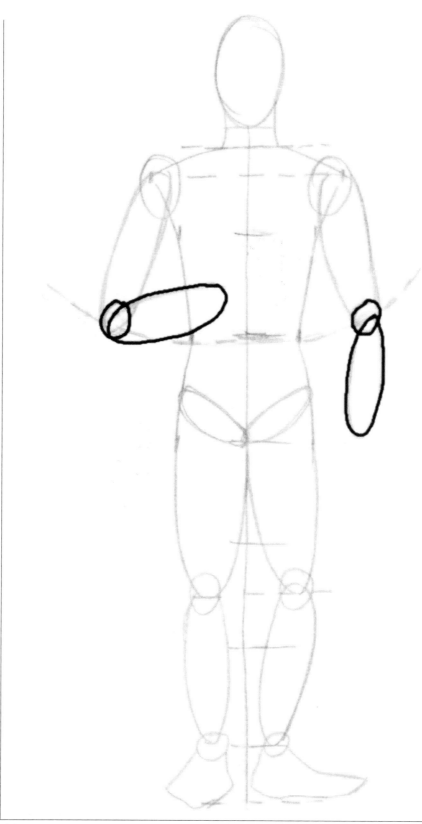

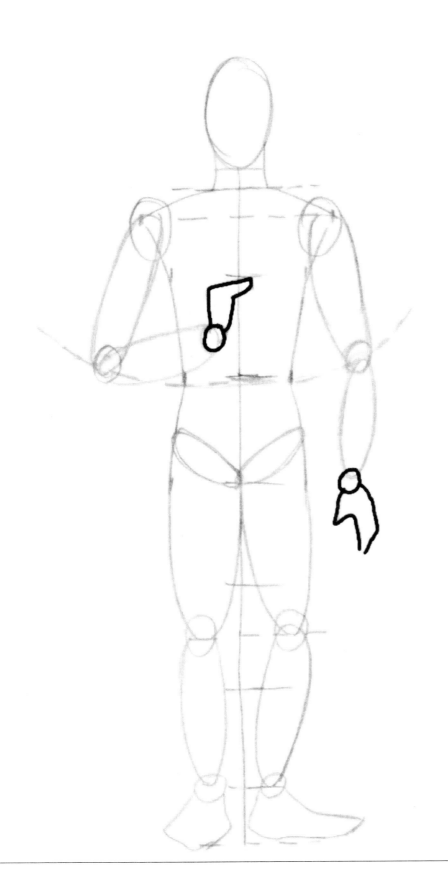

In this preliminary sketch we have not tried to achieve any detailing, only the basic form of the figure. This is the best time to correct any balance or proportions that look a little off.

Now is the time to create a few more of these "glass figures" on your own as practice, with arms and legs in different positions. Remember to always pivot arms and legs from the center of their respective joints and to keep the proportions true. We will discuss gestures and positioning in a later section.

As a further exercise, it is beneficial at this point to take tracing paper and draw these "glass figures" over actual full-length photos of people in magazines and books to see how proportions work and how the body establishes balance with the Plummet Line. Use the photos as a guide as you sketch in the lengths, widths, joints and ovals. It should help you discover how this proportional system relates to the actual human form.

We will learn how to turn the body and work with angles later. At this point, just play with proportions until they make sense. Remember to let proportions be your assistant and not your task master. These are guidelines, not hard rules to follow. Allow these proportional techniques to help in your figure drawing, but don't expect this robotic approach to bring forth natural looking figures immediately. You'll learn to adapt and control this system as you use it more and more.

After all, the best teacher is practice!

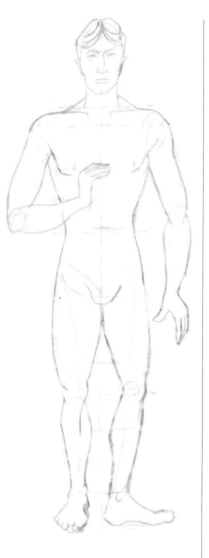

ADDING DETAILS

In this book we take you from head oval to finished, proportional doll...and then we suddenly draw a detailed figure. There obviously seems to be a major step missing in our "step-by-step" approach, but the fact remains that the actual figure drawing techniques used to complete the form could fill volumes by themselves! A good class in figure drawing would be beneficial, and many books are available to offer figure drawing exercises for the student. What is most important to remember is to clean out your old "symbols" and to create new ones by observation and exercise. Learning the actual shape of the human form through bone and muscle layering can be a time consuming study, but any time spent in this area will be richly rewarded. For now, pick up any book that can supply you sketches of the human body, with information on the internal bone and muscle structures. Though you are most interested in the external silhouette, seeing the internal structures will help you understand how the outlines of skin are formed by the complex systems beneath. This is Glass Technique at its finest. When you find areas of the figure that are particularly hard for you to draw, refer to your anatomy reference and sketch the internal bone and muscle layers to more fully understand the external silhouette. Remember, the more you draw, the more you will understand.

Again, as stated in the introduction, I can't emphasize enough the value of creating a Body Morgue of tracings for each area of the body. Find graphic artists' books and trace as much as possible.

Tracing actual photos of human figures can also be beneficial as long as the student remembers that costume design is a graphic art and simple lines are more important than three dimensional pencil sketches. The costume designer has little time to create fully rendered figure drawings when designing a production with well over a hundred costumes. Figures must be produced quickly in simple line form. This means that a good understanding of internal structures is crucial, but silhouette is most important. Clean line drawings will be most beneficial for the final sketch and time saved in drawing the figure will offer time needed in clothing the form and painting the completed sketch.

The keys to figure drawing are practice and patience. Sketch whenever you have free time and practice areas of the body that are hard for you. Most artists will especially find proportions of the opposite sex the hardest to capture. Somehow living "within" one human form helps us understand its proportions better. You will need specific exercises with figures of the opposite sex to capture the male or female proportions you can't "genetically" understand. But above all, practice!

This book can only give you proportional rules to guide your figure drawing. The actual skin silhouettes must come through a personal commitment to learn true body shapes. To aid in your personal study, let us look at some other specific proportional techniques that can help with detailed areas of the body.

*   *   *

At this point, we must note that the female figure is not complete without the addition of breasts. The width proportions we learned were based on bone structure and the female breasts add an entirely new dimension to the female torso. There is also no set proportion for them, as breast size varies widely from person to person. The sizing decision depends much on age, character interpretation and on the actress actually cast in the role, so this becomes a very individual decision.

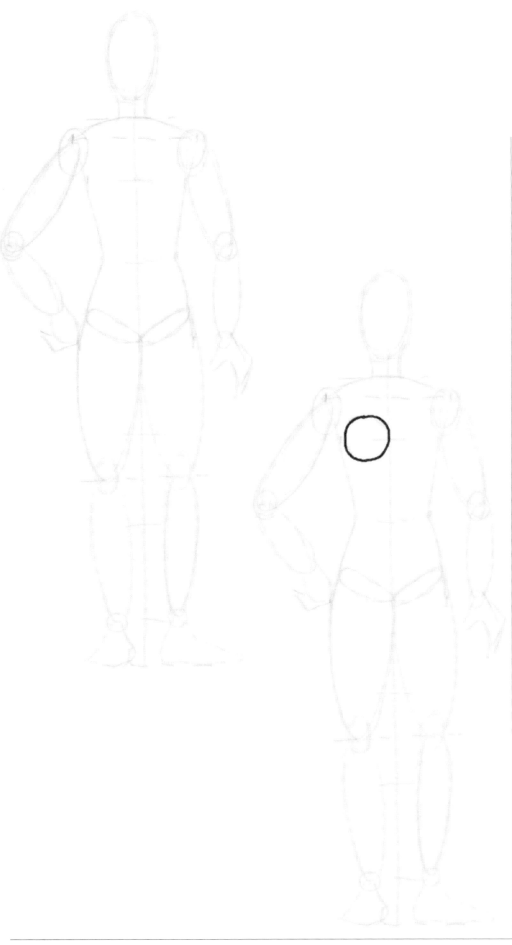

1. Here is a proportional female glass figure. Note the different Head width proportions that make it unique from the male form.

2. In actually drawing the breasts, establish one breast using a simple circle centered vertically on the second Head mark. The circle is simply placed horizontally between the Center Front line and the outer silhouette of the torso. For some female body types, this circle may *increase* the torso proportion. Also, as age increases, the breasts will tend to move down the figure, so the placement oval can be lowered as needed.

3. Now match the other breast with a circle the same dimension on the other side of the chest region.

4. Completing the breast shape has a lot to do with what a figure drawing class and an anatomy book will teach you about actual body line. Generally speaking, use the bottom of each circle to produce the "hang" of the breast, and erase the top of the circle to attach the breast to the form.

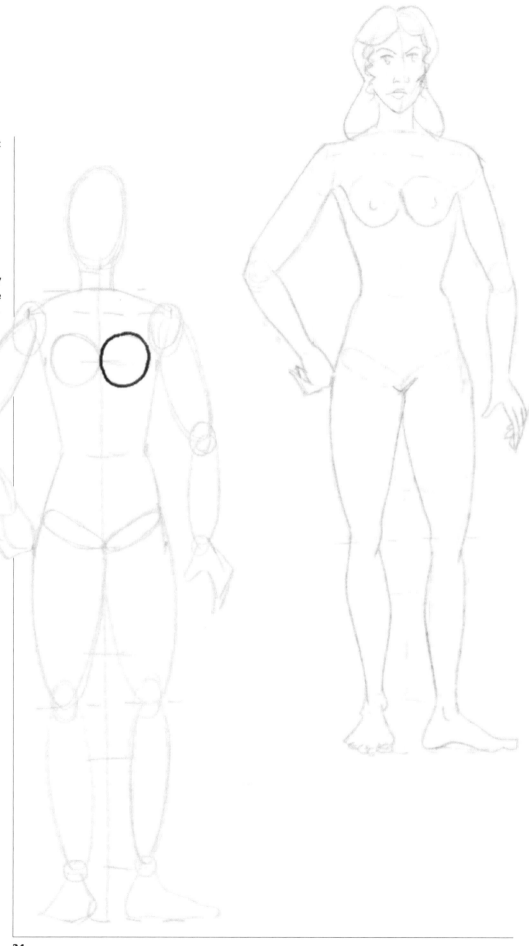

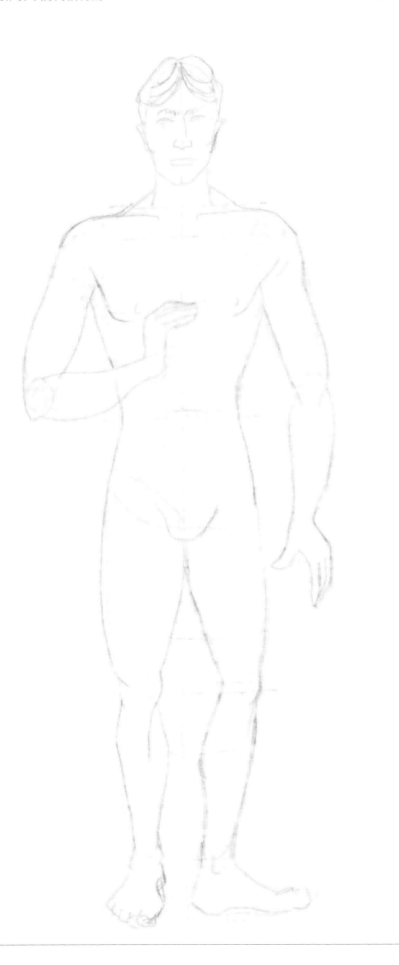

Understanding the dimensional shaping of the male sexual region is really rather basic for the costume designer. Full detailing is not necessary, but an understanding of the additional dimensioning required in some costume pieces is essential.

1. **Generally speaking, the addition of a simple "bag" shape is enough of a graphical representation for the male genitals.**

Let's look now at detailing some of the more complex areas of the human form. The human *face, hands* and *feet* tend to panic even the best artist, but it is important to remember that as a costume designer you are not selling the figure, the figure is selling your costume design. Consequently, the detailing of the figure should not detract from the costume itself. Many students spend too much time on these detail areas of the body and attract the viewers' attention with an over-emphasis in line work. Simple, quick lines are usually the best. Remember, the amount of detail in these areas must balance with the rest of the rendering.

The *face* has its own proportions in relationship to the rest of the body. Let us draw a human head detached from the rest of the figure and enlarge it so we can more fully see the correct proportions.

1. Begin by drawing the head oval. For this exercise, make it between four and five inches tall.

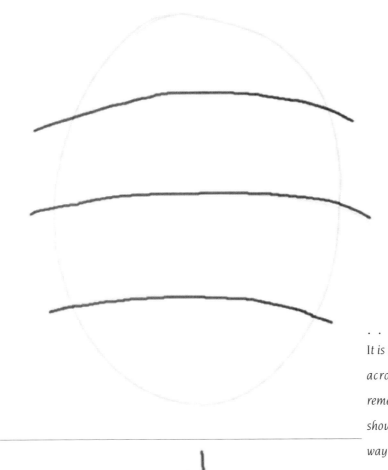

2. As in the illustration, start by dividing the head in half. Then divide the top and bottom sections in half again, creating four equal segments.

. . . .

It is important to note that as we start drawing lines across the human figure anywhere, we must remember that the body is not flat. Therefore all lines should curve to show a dimensional quality . Which way do they curve? Think of your viewing position in relationship to a real body. An area higher than your eye level will curve up, while an area lower than eye level will curve down. You can experiment with different eye levels to see which types of curves produce the best effects.

. . . .

3. Now that the head is cut into quarters, add one more line to mark the Center Front of the face.

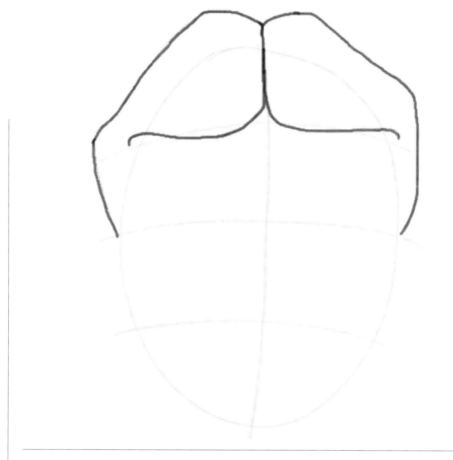

4. Sketch the hair within the top quarter of the head. Remember, hair adds dimension to the head.

The bottom three quarters of the head is the face region. Note in this illustration how the average face is proportionally divided into equal thirds:

a. Hairline to top of nose
b. Top of nose to bottom of nose
c. Bottom of nose to chin.

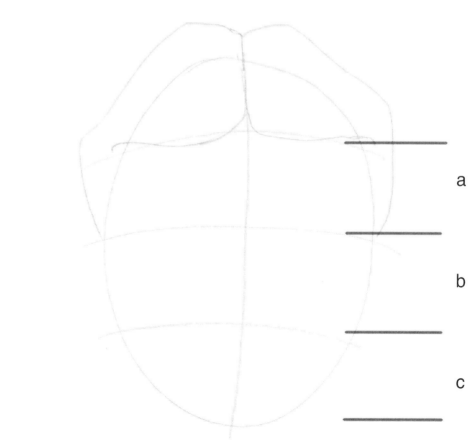

a

b

c

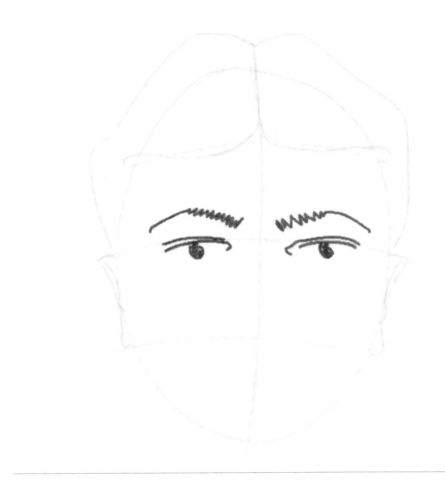

5. Sketch in the eyebrows above the center line and the eyes themselves just below the line, using these width proportions:

a. The eyes are "one eye width" apart.

b. There is roughly "one eye width" from the outside of the head to the eye itself.

6. Sketch in the nose between the marks. Note that the ears also fall within this area, so add them as well.

7. Half way between the nose and the chin is the *bottom* of the lower lip. Sketch in the mouth, noting that its width is generally from "center of eye" to "center of eye."

Practice a few faces on your own. Trace other graphic artists' faces to learn their techniques and add these to your Body Morgue. Here are a few to begin with.

The *Hand* is proportionally the same length as the face (about three-fourths of a Head). Again, we will draw one enlarged to study its proportions.

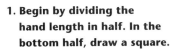
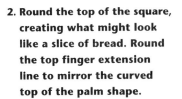

1. **Begin by dividing the hand length in half. In the bottom half, draw a square.**

2. **Round the top of the square, creating what might look like a slice of bread. Round the top finger extension line to mirror the curved top of the palm shape.**

3. **Add the finger ovals up from the top of the palm shape, reaching the curved finger extension line.**

. . . .

Note that the fingers are actually all the same length, except for the little finger, which is generally a bit smaller. And you thought they were all different lengths! They only appear to be different because of the curve at the top of the palm.

. . . .

4. Divide the fingers into thirds with two curved lines. These are the finger joints. We can draw in each individual bone oval if we wish, just to understand how the fingers are constructed.

5. Next, sketch in a "ball" at the inside of the square. This is the thumb joint. The thumb muscle adds a dimensional oval to the side of the palm.

6. From this "ball" sketch the thumb. It extends out to meet the arch of the second finger joint.

7. Divide the thumb in half to find its second joint. The first joint of the thumb is located where it attaches to the "ball."

These proportions can be used to create hands in different positions, but it is a complicated process. Drawing each joint and bone oval is time consuming. A much better approach is to develop your own feel for hand positioning. Begin by tracing other artists' work for your Body Morgue. This will teach you graphical symbols for hands to add to your mental warehouse.

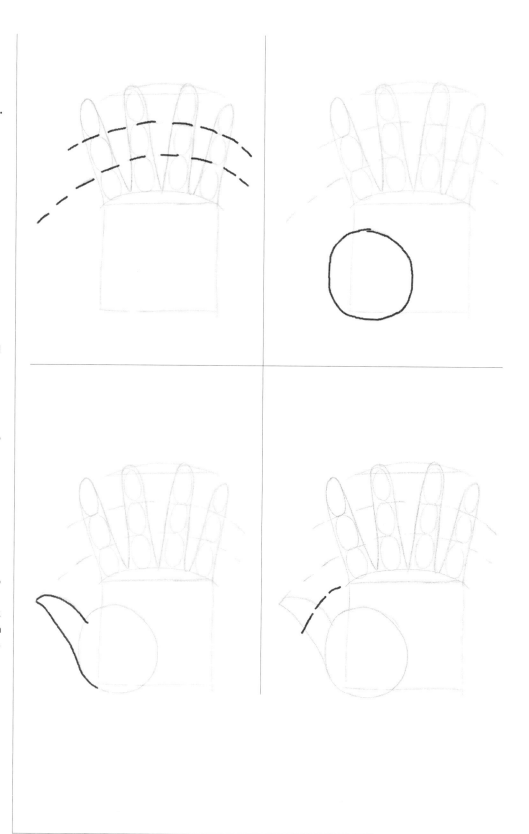

Here is a collection of hands to
begin with.

The *Foot* is complicated only because of the inherent spring of the arch (which in turn gives life to the entire figure.) To more fully understand the proportions, we will draw two feet at the same time, one in side view and one in front view.

1. The ankle connection to the leg is another part of the body's spring system. Sketch the bottom of the leg in both views as illustrated. Don't forget to draw in the Center Front lines as a guide.

Note the leg angles. In the side view the leg bone angles slighting from the knee *backwards* into the ankle.

In the front view the leg angles from the hip *in* to the center of the body, so that each of us is slightly "bow legged" in actual stance. This places the ankles at an angle visible in the front view. Because of this angle, the *inside* ankle is higher than the outside ankle (which explains why you may tend to wear a blister on your *outside* ankle when you break in a new pair of shoes.)

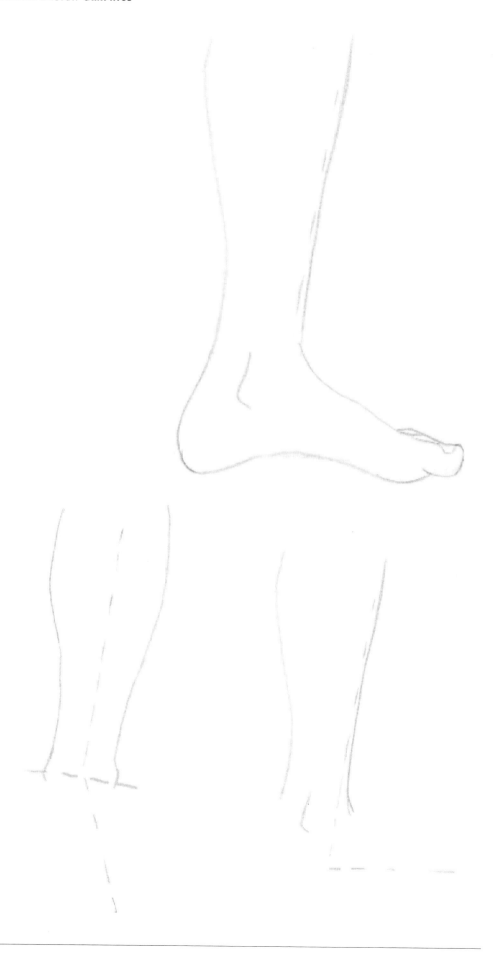

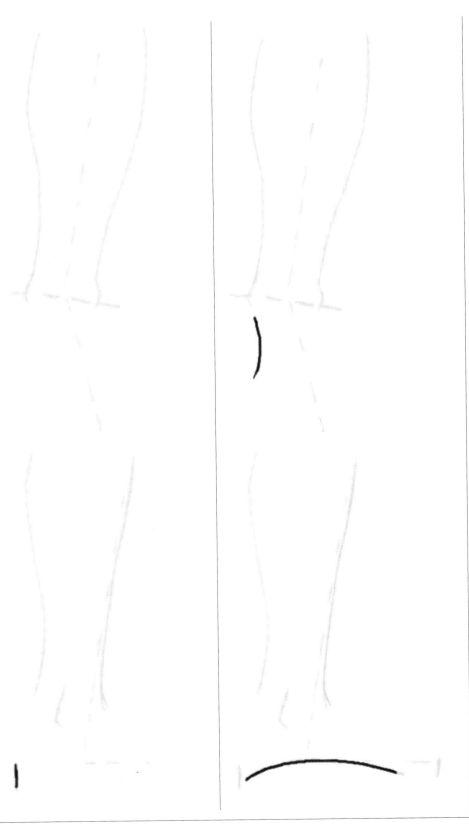

2. **Let's mark one Head in length for the side view. Note that the heel protrudes somewhat from the back of the leg.**

   The front view will be fore-shortened since the foot comes perspectively towards us, so we won't worry about a length mark at this time.

3. **Draw the bottom arch in the side view to capture the animated line of the foot. Note how we also draw the inside of the arch curve in the front view.**

4. The top arch of the foot mirrors the bottom arch. Sketch it in the side view as illustrated.

5. The foot itself is basically a "figure 8" in the side view, with the pads at the heel and ball acting as the two circles.

For the front view, sketch in an "8" to help for placement, overlapping the two circles in Glass Technique.

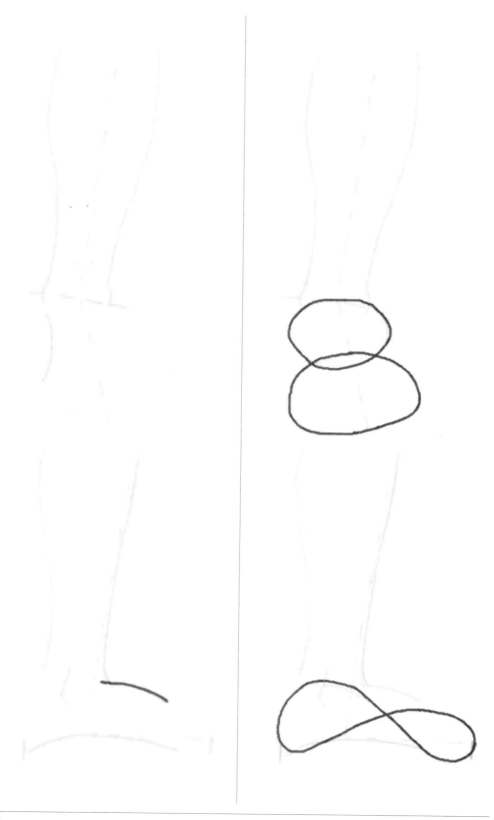

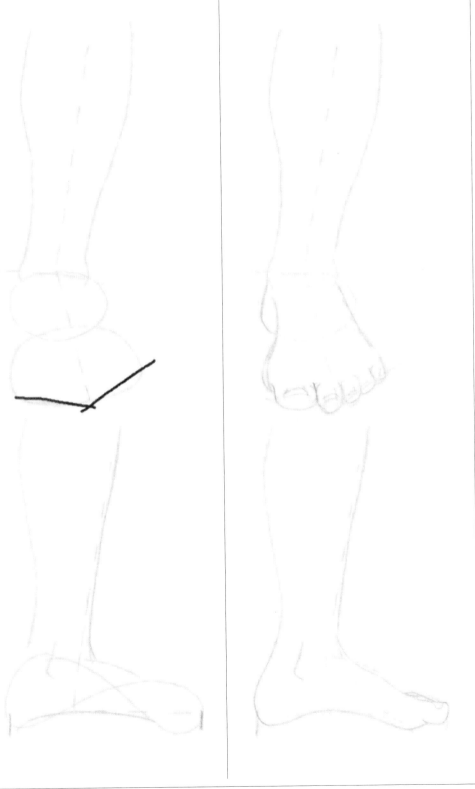

6. **The foot tends to point toward the second toe. Mark this point with two lines in the front view.**

7. **Sketch each view of the foot within the guidelines.**

Feet are not as proportionally defined as other body areas, so tracing is perhaps the best way to learn how to draw them. Keep the angles and basic shaping ideas in mind as you work.

Here are a few feet to begin your
Body Morgue.

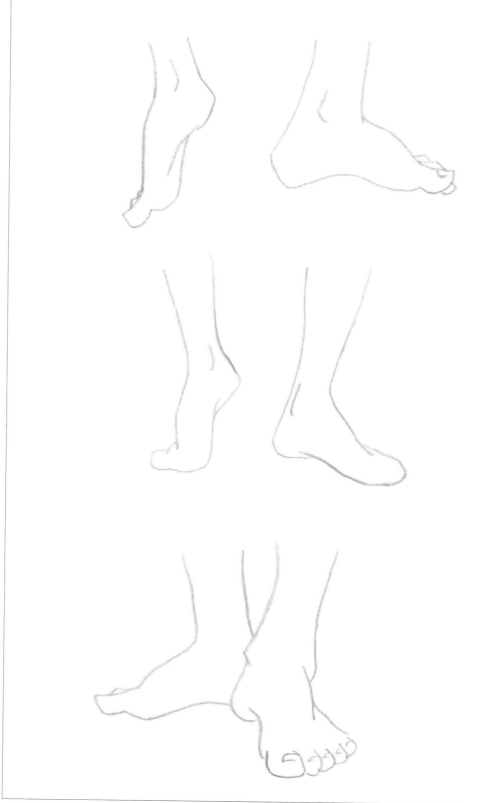

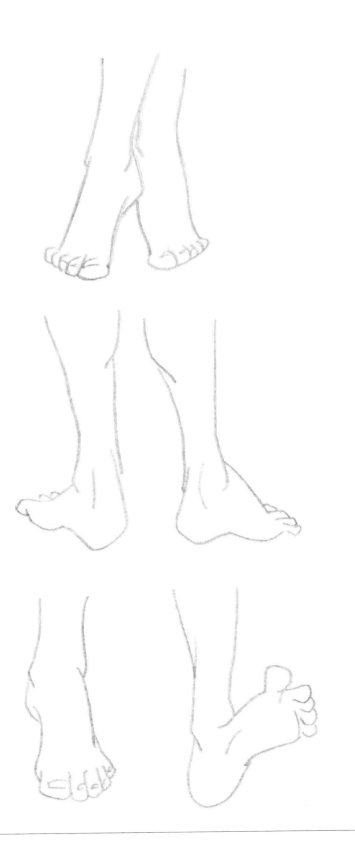

These detailing exercises have helped us see that shaping is important. We convey external shape by remembering the true shape of the internal. To reiterate, in your drawing exercises as you reach areas of the body you don't quite understand, research and draw them in their skeletal and muscular form first. The process should help you better understand their external line. This approach (the Glass Technique) teaches you to forget the external structure until the internal structure is correct. We will continue to use this technique in later exercises.

In actuality, the human body is hardest to draw in full front view. The "three-quarters view" is not only easier, but it is also more pleasing in composition and more efficient in expressing body movement. The application of proportions is entirely the same, except for the width placements along the Center Front line. The term three-quarters will become more apparent as we draw, but basically understand the approach as drawing a figure turned slightly to one side.

Let us try drawing a male figure in three-quarters view. We will follow the same basic steps used in drawing a front view.

1. **We begin by drawing the head oval and the Head lengths for placement.**

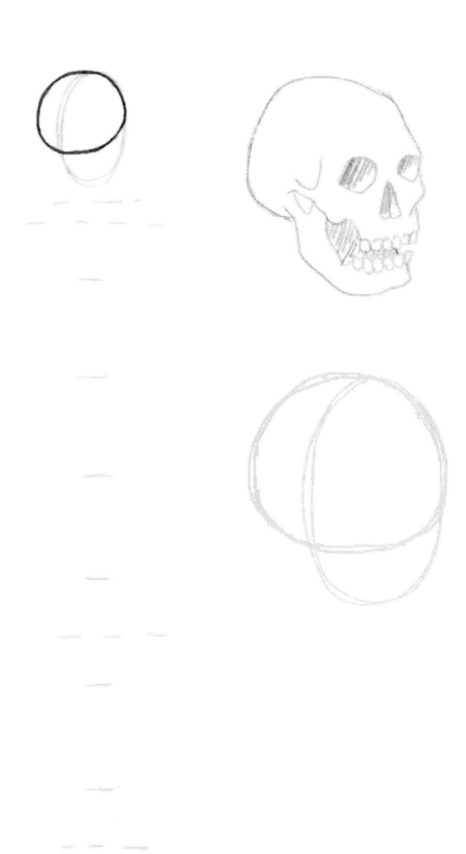

2. At this point, we find our first change. Once the head is turned at an angle it is no longer a simple oval but is now *two* interlocking ovals. The second oval is more circular than the first and extends two-thirds the way down the first oval (to about the tip of the nose). Compare the two ovals to the human skull in this illustration and you should be able to see how the two ovals complete the general shape.

3. **Mark the Center Front of the head now. In any angled view, keeping track of the Center Front line is very important.**

4. **Now we must sketch in the neck. We did this later on in the front view, but neck angle is essential is capturing the three-quarters view.**

You may want to look at a few graphic drawings or photos to see the neck angle. Make sure you understand that the human neck *does not* run in a straight, vertical line down from the head in side view. This could be a good time to stand in front of the mirror and see how the neck sets the head somewhat forward from the rest of the body.

Note that the physical center of the neck cylinder can be found by drawing a line from the Center Front top of the front oval down through the bottom intersection of the two ovals.

. . . .

Note that we use a curved line for dimension and that the Center Front line is not in the "true" center of the ovals, but signifies the head turned slightly to the side. In actuality, about one-quarter of the head width is on one side of the Center Front line and the remaining three-quarter of the head width is on the other side. This is where the term "three-quarters view" comes from.

. . . .

5. Sketch in the Center Front line of the neck. Remember that it divides the neck itself into the same one-quarter/ three-quarter relationship we used on the head.

6. At this point, a new line becomes important to us: the Center Front body line.

But wait! Didn't we use one in the front figure and call it the "Plummet Line?" Yes, actually we did. In a front view, the Center Front line and the Plummet Line overlap and are represented by one line only, but they are *separate* lines in an angled view.

Note that the line is drawn in a curve from the bottom of the Center Front neck line (on your own body this would be the point at the top of your chest just at the base of your throat) and runs through the chest and waist marks, stopping at the crotch.

Again, the use of a curved line adds dimension to the body.

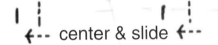

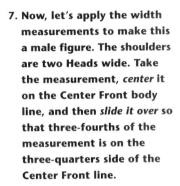

7. Now, let's apply the width measurements to make this a male figure. The shoulders are two Heads wide. Take the measurement, *center* it on the Center Front body line, and then *slide it over* so that three-fourths of the measurement is on the three-quarters side of the Center Front line.

8. Mark the chest width by taking a $1^1/_2$ Heads measurement, centering it on the Center Front body line and then sliding it over to the three-quarters side.

9. **Follow the same process to find the marks for the waist (1$^1/_4$ Heads wide) and the hips (1$^1/_2$ Heads wide).**

10. **Connecting these marks begins to expose the angled body view. Note how flat the one-quarter side becomes and how the curve of the back is shown on the three-quarters side.**

Look in a mirror at your three-quarter view and see how your silhouette lines follow these same rules.

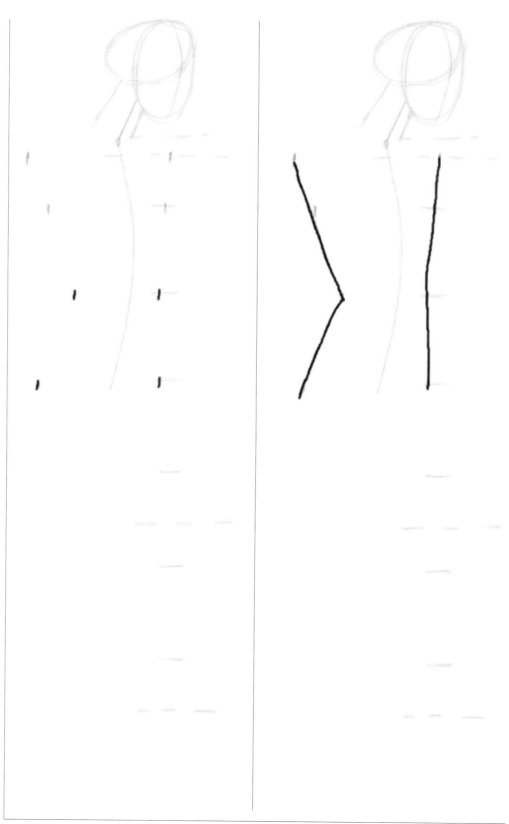

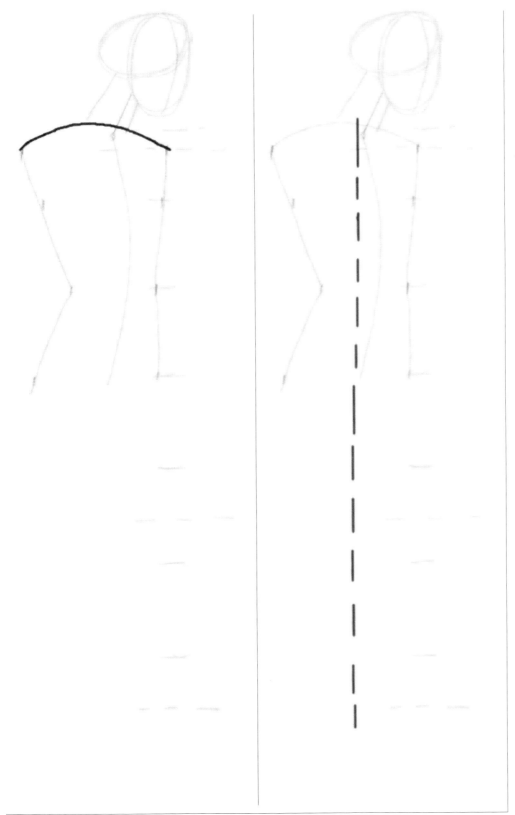

11. **Draw in a connecting curve for the shoulder line up to the neck. At this point, it will appear to be a little clumsy, but we will clean it up later.**

12. ***Now* it is time to add the Plummet Line to find the center of gravity for the figure. This line is a straight vertical dropped from the "physical center" of the bottom of the neck (a point half way from side to side *and* front to back).**

Look at this illustration to locate the point:

Simply drop a straight line from this neck point to the "ground." This marks the center of gravity for the body.

13. **Let us draw the shoulder joints next. They are the same circles we drew in the front view with one minor change. In the front view the joints *added* dimension to the human form, extending the shoulder measurement. In the three-quarters view these joints are drawn *within* the shoulder markings.**

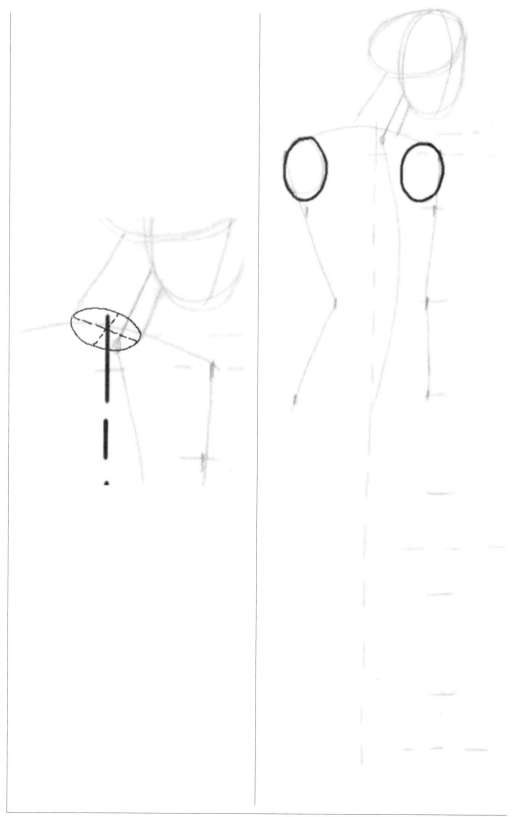

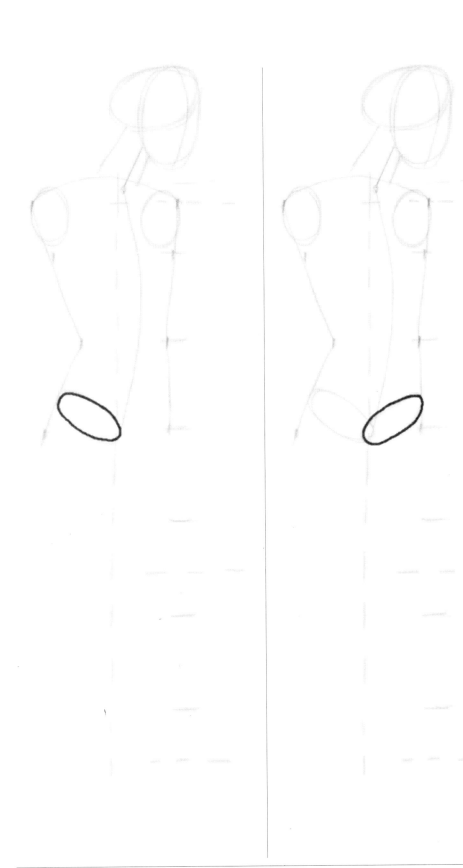

In real life, we would not be able to see the joint on the opposite side of the body, but we will use the Glass Technique and sketch it in so that *both* shoulder joints are visible. This will be important for correct arm placement.

14. **The hip "butterfly" is a bit more complicated when drawn at an angle. Begin with the joint on the three-quarter measurement side of the figure. Draw in the flattened oval from the hip down to the crotch mark, creating the "panty line."**

15. **Take a measurement from this hip oval and transfer it to the other hip (angling it in the opposite direction). Using the Glass Technique, sketch it in, overlapping the other hip joint.**

If you could look through your own body, these ovals would be true to the effect of looking through one joint and seeing the other.

16. **Now it is time to draw in the appendages. Let us begin with the arm** *away* **from you (on the opposite side of the body). Draw in the upper arm using the "shoulder point to waist" measurement as before, and apply the measurement down and out from the shoulder joint. Draw in the oval, using the entire shoulder joint circle for the connection.**

17. **Sketch in the elbow joint as before if you wish. Now use the "waist to crotch" measurement to measure the lower arm out from the center of the elbow joint.**

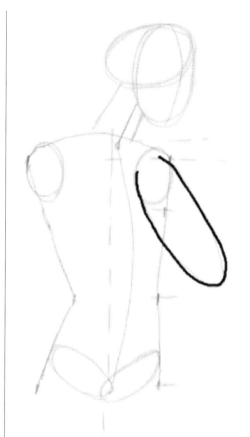
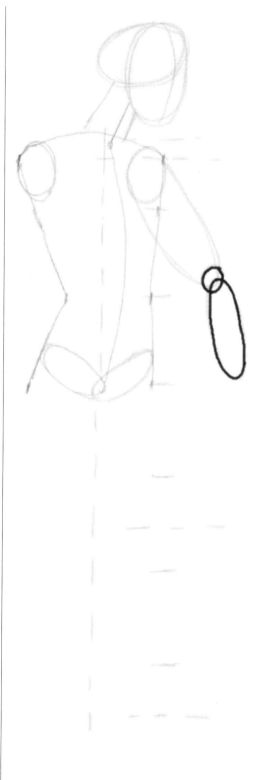

. . . .

Remember, you can "swing" arm measurements out any direction you wish from the center of the joints, keeping in mind the physical restrictions of the human body. If you want to know the restrictions, try to bend your own arm into the desired angle. If you can't do it, then don't draw it!

. . . .

18. Sketch a quick hand. You can detail it later.

19. Draw in the other complete arm, using the same process.

20. Let us now sketch the legs. We must remember the gravity rules and keep the Plummet Line *within* the inside ankles of the two feet. Sketch in the upper leg on the far side of the body (making sure to use the *entire* hip joint at the top) and stop at the knee mark.

21. **Add a knee joint. Drop a Center Front line to mark the placement of the shin bone and sketch in the lower leg oval.**

22. **Repeat the process for the other leg. Note that the thighs will *overlap* in the three-quarters view.**

23. **Add feet for support. Note that the foot on the three-quarter side has been fore-shortened as it perspectively points at the viewer.**

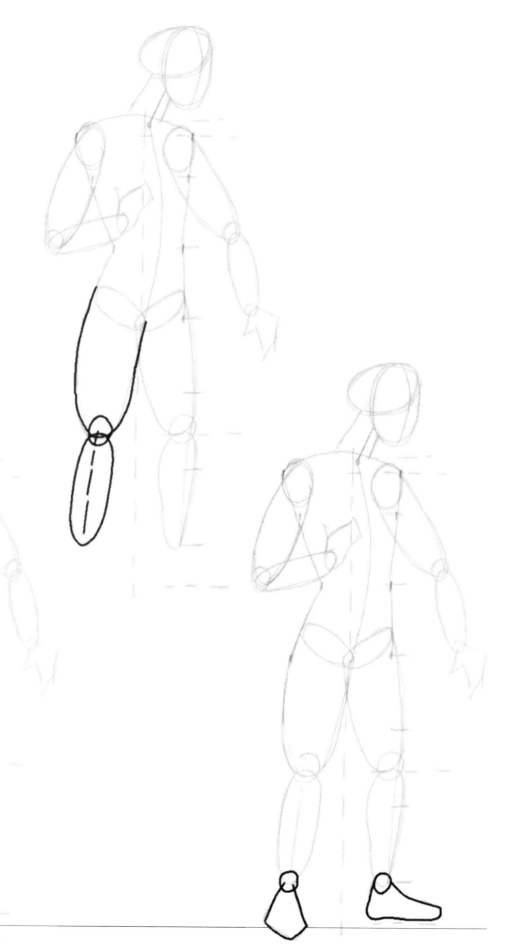

24. Erase all the hidden lines and a figure will appear.

25. Now comes the hard part. Apply the body shapes you have studied *over* the glass figure. In the illustration, compare the glass figure with that of the finished figure to see dimension now at work.

Before we leave this process, let us experiment with leg placement.

1. **In this illustration we have drawn in the first leg. Note that according to the rules of gravity this figure should be able to stand on *one* foot. Let us place the other leg off in a strong angle. We have to remember that the leg can not be *elongated*, but has to stay in the same proportions.**

2. **The easiest way to accomplish this is to take a measurement from the upper leg we have already drawn. Now pivot that measurement out from the other hip joint.**

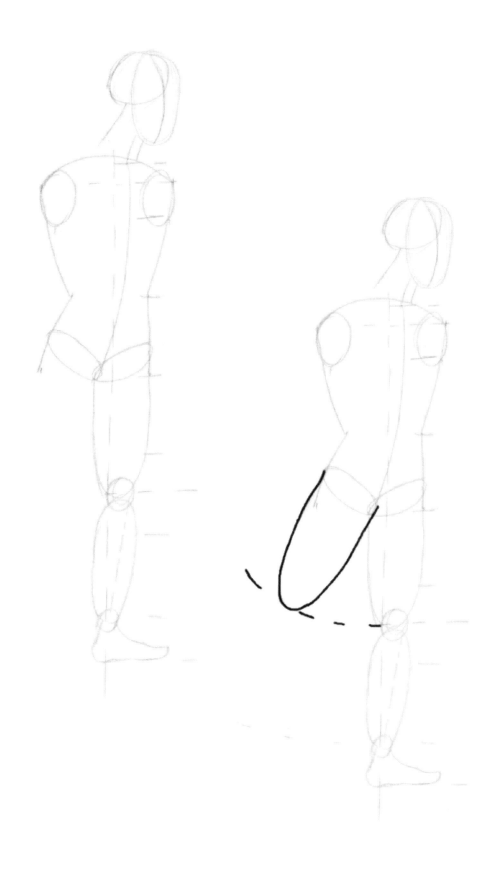

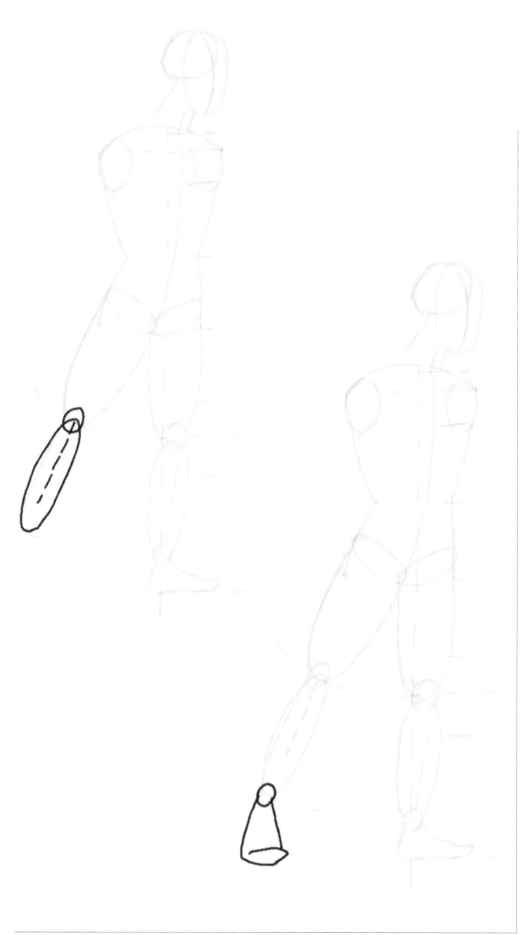

3. We now sketch in the knee joint and take a measurement from the lower leg already sketched. We apply that measurement out and find that we don't quite reach the floor in this angle...

4. ...so we have to sketch an extended foot to reach to the ground. It is usually a good idea to use a mirror to study a particular stance before you attempt it on paper.

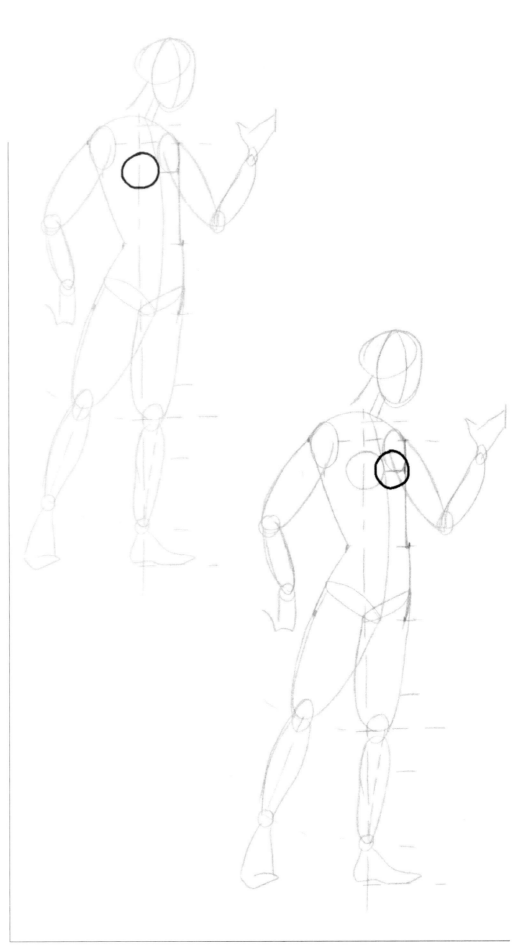

One last three-quarters study we need to make is a female figure.

1. **We have drawn the basic figure here but need to add the dimensional shaping of the breasts. Begin with the breast on the "three-quarters" side. Draw in the size of circle desired, touching the Center Front body line and centering it vertically on the bust point mark.**

2. **Take a measurement from this circle and draw the other breast** *behind* **the first, positioned proportionally with the one-quarter side of the body. This may take some practice but the object is to make sure the breast is the** *same size.* **Be sure not to crunch it into the area remaining. Use the Glass Technique to place it correctly.**

3. In this illustration, we have removed hidden lines and completed the breasts, showing the angled shapes.

Practice a few three-quarters figures until you feel comfortable sliding width proportions over to the three-quarters side and drawing the Center Front body line at different angles. Some beginning students tend to lose the three-quarters side of the body. Remember, once you have drawn in the Center Front line for the head, you have established the three-quarters side.

Here are a few examples of some possible variations of body place-ment. Let us also mention at this point that "three-quarters" is only a term. Some of these figures are turned more than others, so that "three-fifths" or "one-quarter" might be a more appropriate term. The degree of rotation is entirely up to you as the designer. Simply stay true to the amount you slide the proportions over from the Center Front line and the figure should stay proportionally correct.

. . . .

We must also keep in mind that the human body is generally wider than it is thick. What this means is that if we turned the body completely sideways we could not use the male and female width ratios to draw the shoulder, chest, waist and hip areas. We must also realize that as we rotate the figure into extreme angled views we will begin to lose some width in the realized figure. Don't let this throw you in the techniques we have just used. Study some actual bodies and apply the Head measurements to see the amount of width proportions lost for different angles. The same effect can be achieved if, when you are applying width proportions to mark widths, you simply move in the marks a fraction. A lot of this simply has to do with your own perception. Learn to trust your eye as you draw. If a figure seems too wide, move the marks in a bit to help the look. Remember, nothing we have applied here is a rule of the universe! Use the technique; don't allow it to use you. It is meant as a guide to proportion only. It will never replace actual drawing practice with a real human form as you study true proportions in different stances.

. . . .

Now that proportions are understood, the figure can be animated. As we create movement in the figure's stance, remember to keep the Plummet Line in tact so the figure will remain in balance.

At this point let us render the body in solid shapes so that we understand which areas are flexible and which areas are not. The illustration shows a proportioned body with all parts drawn in "block shapes." These blocks are not considered flexible and must move as one entire piece. (In actuality, the torso block *is* semi-flexible along the spinal cord and some distortion within this region is possible, but we still must think of this area as one unit.) Note particularly the torso and hip units and how they move in relationship to each other. The waist joint keeps these two shapes together and any movement must be within the logical rotation of this joint.

Note this example of torso contortion and how the waist joint is used to roll the shapes about.

The next illustrations demonstrate contortions of the full body. Note that all parts rotate on their individual joints. Note also that either one inside ankle or a combination of both ankles must fall within the gravity line to balance each figure.

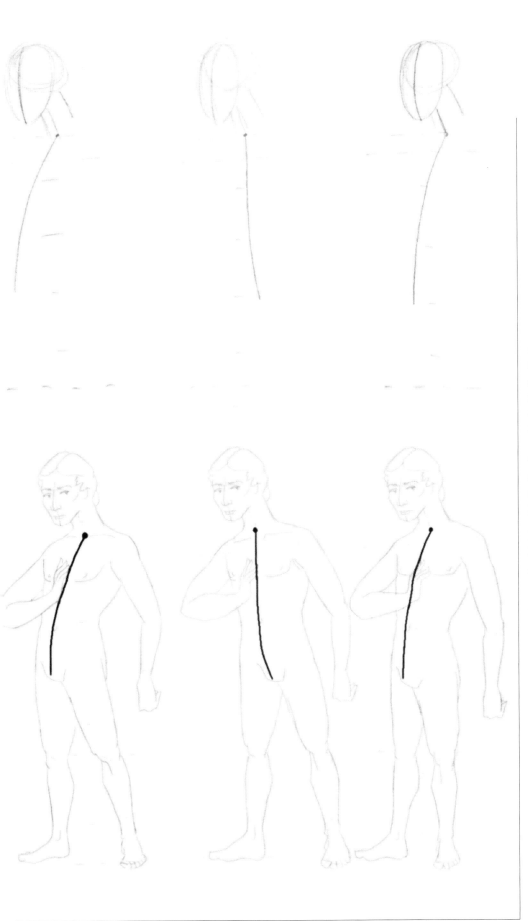

In creating a moving figure, we start with the head shape and the neck attached. All Head lengths are marked for the body sketch-in. Before we draw the torso, we must draw in the Center Front body line and use it to help in the contortion.

These illustrations show variations of the Center Front body line and the figure completed to fit the contortion. Note that the Center Front line must be in correct proportion, stopping at the crotch point. Eventually you will be able to sense the correct proportion of this line and know where the bust point, waist and hip placement fall along its length. For now, just be mindful of the Head marks as you draw.

Here are several bodies in motion. Study their skeletal roots and the exterior detailing.

DESIGNING THE NUDE

The figure on which the costume design is displayed has as much or more to do with the selling of the design than the costume itself. Because of this, it is important that the designer creates the correct nude figure for the character on which the costume design can then be better represented. And since each character tends to develop within a script, one figure for all of a character's costumes is rarely adequate. The nude must express the character in each step of development, as such representation is essential in selling the costume design itself.

Designing the correct nude is an art in itself. No costume can ever look good if the figure beneath is incorrect. It is vital to the overall design that the costume designer knows the figure beneath and creates it before any costume piece is drawn.

In approaching the design of a nude, some philosophy of stance is necessary. In our modern theatre art form we stress the realistic style of acting. Indeed we even make fun of some of the earlier techniques studied by actors to "represent" life rather than "present" it. However, in the representational art form of costume design, character interpretation through the silent stance of graphic figures has little to do with realism. Therefore, we can use the theories of early acting stance for great effect in our renderings.

Many of the theories these earlier performers used were based heavily upon the teachings of Francois Delsarte. This book cannot begin to cover the entire teachings of Delsarte, but we can glean an overall theory of stance from his work. Delsarte was an oratorical instructor of the late 1800s who noticed that stance not only influences a speaker's vocal projection but

it can also influence the way in which an audience perceives the visual character.

We are interested in some of Delsarte's general approaches of body division and balance, since these ideas are quite effective in two-dimensional figure communication. Realize that much of what Delsarte taught came from his study of statuary, and in many ways our costume designs directly relate to this form of art.

One of the first basics of Delsarte's theory was the division of the body into three parts. The illustration shows the main divisions and their dominant characteristics. These "regions" are meaningless to us in theory, but are actually very effective in practice. To demonstrate the use of this theory let us try a simple experiment.

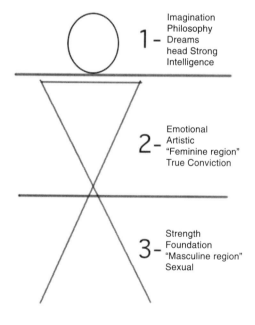

1 – Imagination
Philosophy
Dreams
head Strong
Intelligence

2 – Emotional
Artistic
"Feminine region"
True Conviction

3 – Strength
Foundation
"Masculine region"
Sexual

Use the simple phrase "I love you." Stand in front of a mirror so that your full form is visible. With both hands held up in the first region, speak the phrase. You will undoubtedly feel as the poet or philosopher and almost begin to break into verse: "How do I love thee, let me count the ways!"

Now drop your hands into the second region and speak the phrase again. The words cannot help but be more sincere in this emotional region. Here is the lover's true area of expression. When we wish to imply that someone is extremely committed to some belief we tend to state that his or her *heart* is set upon it.

Therefore, this is the region of true conviction and decision, while the first region merely supports a theoretical or philosophical approach.

Drop the hands further into the third region below the waist and utter the phrase again. You will sense the sexual nature of the phrase. This area expresses an almost animalistic side of human communication. Delsarte labels this "vulgar expression," though not at all referring to our modern connotation of the term. He simply infers the "common" or "typical" and therefore the "animal instinct" of man.

Refer now to these illustrations. The figures are identical except for arm placement. Note the difference these regions can make in body communication.

Two other theories of Delsarte are applicable to the nude figure. First, the wider the base of the figure, the stronger the resolve and apparent power the figure possesses. "Base" refers to the foundation of the body in the lower masculine region, where strength is a dominant characteristic. It more specifically applies to the gravitational spread of the feet. A figure with feet apart will have a stronger foundation than a figure whose feet are closer together. Simply stated, it is easy to push over a figure with a narrower base. Compare the figures in the illustration and note the difference in strength expressed by the varying base stances.

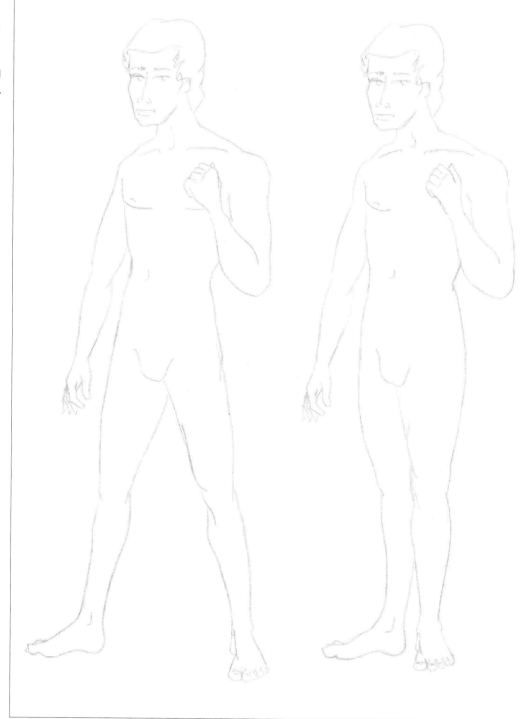

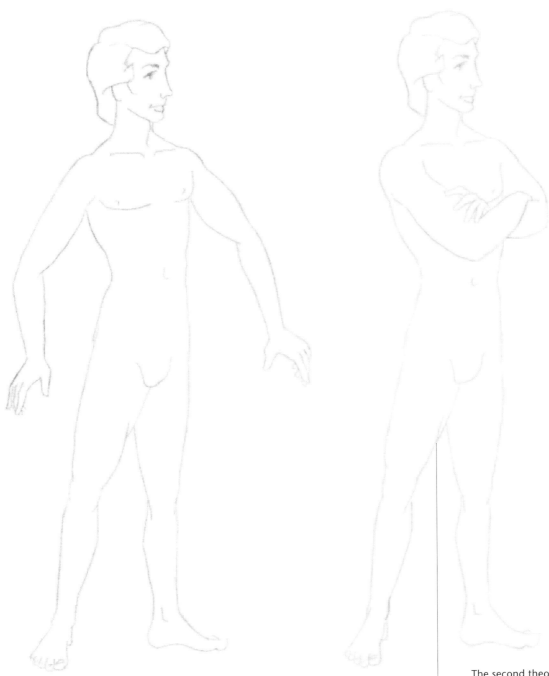

The second theory from which we can benefit is the closed and open positioning of the figure in general. As a figure "closes" itself off with the arms or any other part of the body, the figure will appear "less vulnerable," somewhat hesitant and possibly even secretive. In opposition to this, a figure whose arms are spread away from the body or whose entire body is clearly revealed will appear "vulnerable." Again refer to the illustrations as examples of this theory.

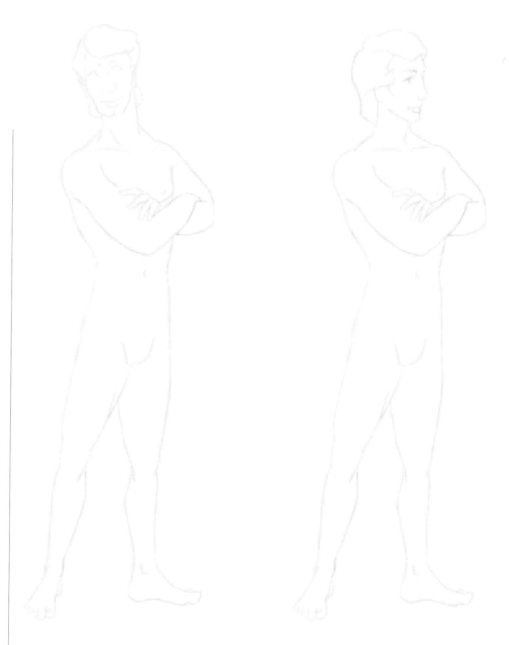

The *face* itself can communicate much about "openness" of character. The more the face is turned towards the viewer the more we expect the character to reveal. In contrast, the more the face turns away, the more secretive and underhanded the character becomes. Note these figures and how much difference the head itself can make.

The last in our study in Delsarte's approaches is perhaps a bit more involved. Delsarte outlined the possible stances of the feet in comparison to the balance of the body above them and found that each position tended to denote specific characteristics. We can basically stand with our weight evenly on both feet or shift all of our weight onto one foot. While in either stance we can distribute our weight to 1) the ball of the foot, 2) the middle or the foot, or 3) the heel of the foot.

Below is a chart created from Delsarte's approach showing these positioning factors and the characteristics of each. Stand up and try them yourself to see how they actually apply to the way you feel in each stance.

Application of this theory of stance is a little complicated, but very effective. As you approach a character, refer to Delsarte's chart and circle the adjectives that apply to the character at a particular moment in the script. You will usually find your character falls in a general category, such as a "front foot character" or an "even-balanced character." There are many variations, but look for the common balance stance you find through the adjectives selected.

weight distributed on:	HEEL	MIDDLE	BALL
BACK FOOT	prostration fatigue	concentrated thinking mental response	defiance active resentment
BOTH	respect servitude	ease (vulgar ease)	uncertainty indecision
FRONT FOOT	suspense anxiety	animation exuberance	vital or explosive response

For an example, let us consider the character of Hamlet. First of all, we must decide what part of the show we are discussing. For this exercise we will choose Act III, Scene II: the scene in which Hamlet has requested a band of players to reenact the murder of his father to see how his uncle, King Claudius, will react. Refer to Delsarte's chart and circle the characteristics of Hamlet for this scene.

Note that our choices make Hamlet a "front foot" and "ball" personality for this scene. Now let us use these balance ideas to create the nude.

First of all, we need to draw the head. But before we go too far, we have a decision to make. Do we face Hamlet left or right on the page? And what difference does it make anyway?

weight distributed on:	HEEL	MIDDLE	BALL
BACK FOOT	prostration fatigue	concentrated thinking mental response	defiance active resentment
BOTH	respect servitude	ease (vulgar ease)	uncertainty indecision
FRONT FOOT	suspense anxiety	animation exuberance	vital or explosive response

Graph reproduced from "It's How You Say It" by Jean R. Jenkins. All rights reserved.

So, with an understanding of direction in mind, and assuming we are in a Western state of mind, let us decide Hamlet's placement. If he faces right (so that he is in effect traveling left to right) he is "with the flow" and has a strong movement capability.

If, in contrast, he faces left, we will find that he appears more head strong and "against the flow." This description seems to support the underlying foundation of Hamlet throughout most of the play, does it not?

Let us position Hamlet facing left, "against the flow."

The differences in directional perception are quite large. Each of us has been trained from birth to see our world in a particular direction. The Western world has learned to see left to right, the direction we read. Wouldn't that infer that the Eastern world might see things in the opposite direction? Of course it does! In fact, compare Western and Eastern art and you will find directional emphasis in direct opposition. The power of direction is truly quite incredible!

1. **Sketch in the head with the double ovals, mark off the Head measurements and sketch in the neck. Make sure to mark the Center Front lines for the head and neck. At this point, we have our second character decision to make. We need to sketch in the Center Front body line.**

We may want to reflect on some acting theory. Characters are "pulled" by areas of their bodies. Review Delsarte's three major regions and ask yourself what "pulls" Hamlet? Is he driven by his intellect, his heart, or his lusts?

Yes. Hamlet appears to be driven by all three at different moments in the play. But what about this particular scene? You may need to talk with the director to make these types of decisions. Costume design is very closely related to acting, and as you "play" each scene for each character, you need to understand how the director envisions the progression.

For our exercise, let us suggest that this is Hamlet's most blatantly sexual scene (or at least he uses his attraction to Ophelia as catalyst for his actions.)

2. **We will draw in the Center Front line from the bottom of the neck, extending its proper length, with its most "forward" position in Delsarte's third region. Placement of this line shows Hamlet's sexual driving force for the scene.**

3. Now, let us draw the three-
   quarters view torso marks,
   applying the widths and
   sliding them over from the
   Center Front line. We con-
   nect the lines to find the
   basic torso and draw in the
   shoulder curve.

4. We next draw in the joints
   and the Plummet Line.

As we approach the legs, let us refer to the Delsarte chart on which we circled Hamlet's characteristics. We have found him to be "forward/ball" in personality.

We also must decide on his "foundation strength." There seems to be great strength in almost everything Hamlet does, so let us keep the foundation rather strong (which means keeping the feet spread widely).

5. With "forward/ball" and "strong foundation" in mind, let us sketch in the legs.

Note how pulling the legs back enough so that the Plummet Line falls toward the front of the supporting ankle pulls the figure's weight forward onto the ball of the front foot. Also note how the extension of the back leg widens the base for us.

We now need arms. Here is another chance for us to make some character decisions. We have given Hamlet a strong sexual "pull" for the scene, but the arms give us a chance to further round out that statement.

In fact, the arms allow us to make two statements if we wish. The front-most arm (because it is closer to the viewer) will be more "obvious" in nature, and can therefore make a strong "external" character statement. The back-most arm (because it is farther from the viewer) is less apparent and can make a more subtle "internal" statement.

Let us play up Hamlet's internal struggle of devotion and loyalty but suggest this is something he wishes to keep to himself.

6. **Using the back arm we will sketch in a second region placement. This arm also closes off Hamlet's true conviction to some degree.**

7. **Hamlet is also rather "preachy" in this scene, so we will place the more obvious arm in the first region to show his philosophical tendencies. Keeping the arm away from the body makes Hamlet vulnerable philosophically.**

8. Here is the completed figure. Note how each figure placement decision adds to the overall effect of figure communication.

Here are two other interpretations for Hamlet in other scenes from the play. One is for Act I, Scenes IV & V: the first ghost segment when Hamlet is most vulnerable in the heart region.

The other is for Act V, Scene I: the scene in which he leaps into Ophelia's grave and challenges Laertes. Can you tell which figure is for which scene?

For practice, design nude figures for two more of Shakespeare's characters as described below and then compare your interpretations with these two illustrations.

A. Design Juliet from *Romeo and Juliet*, Act II, Scene II. The setting is the balcony where Juliet reveals her internal emotions. She feels an internal struggle of devotion for her family and a strong love for Romeo simultaneously.

B. Design Katherine from *The Taming of the Shrew*, Act IV, Scene I. The scene takes place after the wedding ceremony in the home of Petruchio. Katherine has just been married and harbors some inner love for this dashing gentleman. At the same time she shows an outward disdain for the male population as a whole.

As you approach these techniques for creating the nude figure, you will see the myriad of combinations possible between weight/ balance, arm positioning and foundation. We can create a figure tailored especially to any character, in any scene, in any given play.

But be careful! This technique can become mechanical if it is approached too clinically. Trust your instincts. Rely on that human ability to "feel" the personality for each character. Review the charts, mentally noting the meaning of stance, foundation and positioning, and these ideas will become a part of you. Go back to the charts and diagrams only when you have problems and need them to help analyze.

Practice. Draw. Try out these techniques and make them your own. Style is something each designer will find in his or her own way. Never settle into one technique; keep your mind open to *all* techniques. Communication through a pencil is a life-time pursuit, not something to be mastered in one night, one week or even one year.

Our drawing of figures up to this point has assumed that most characters are of average weight and are fully grown adults. This, of course, is far from the truth. The mere fact that we use the word "character" to describe a personality in a script underlines theatre's very unique individuals who, in turn, have very individual physiques.

We must now consider different ages and how Head proportions vary. The typical human being begins as an infant, with a 3 to 4 Head stature and slowly progresses into the $7\frac{1}{2}$ Head ratio which we have discussed up to this point. To draw juvenile or adolescent figures, we will have to look at new proportions.

These illustrations present varying developmental stages of the male and female form in correct lengths and widths for your reference.

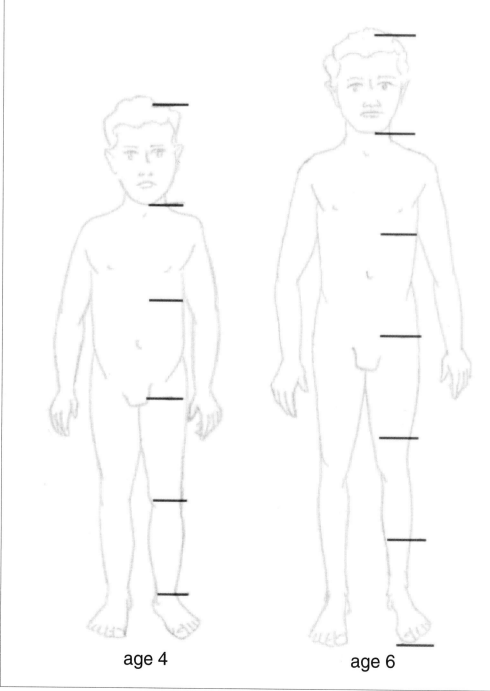

age 4   age 6

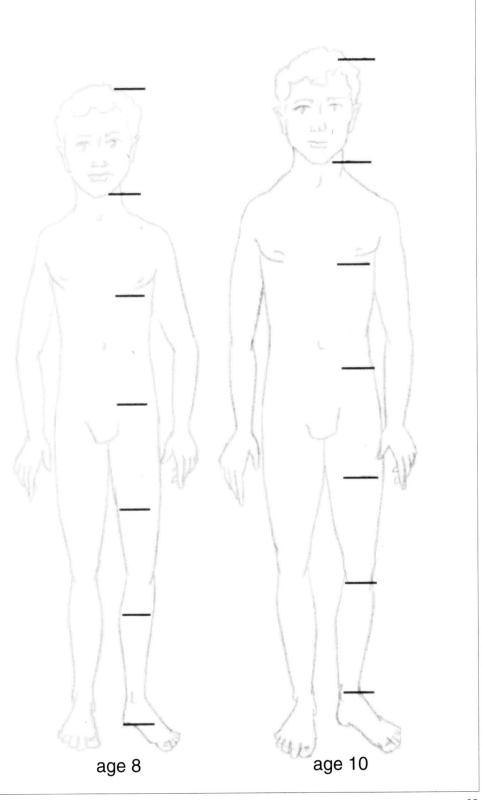

age 8   age 10

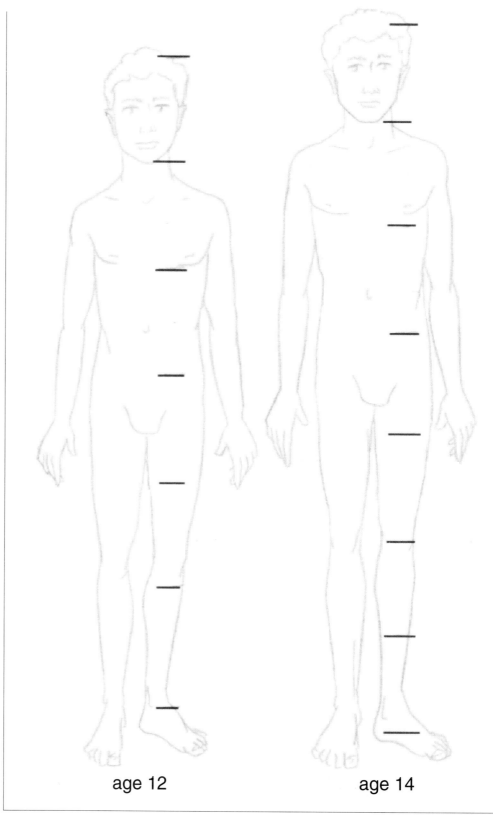

age 12   age 14

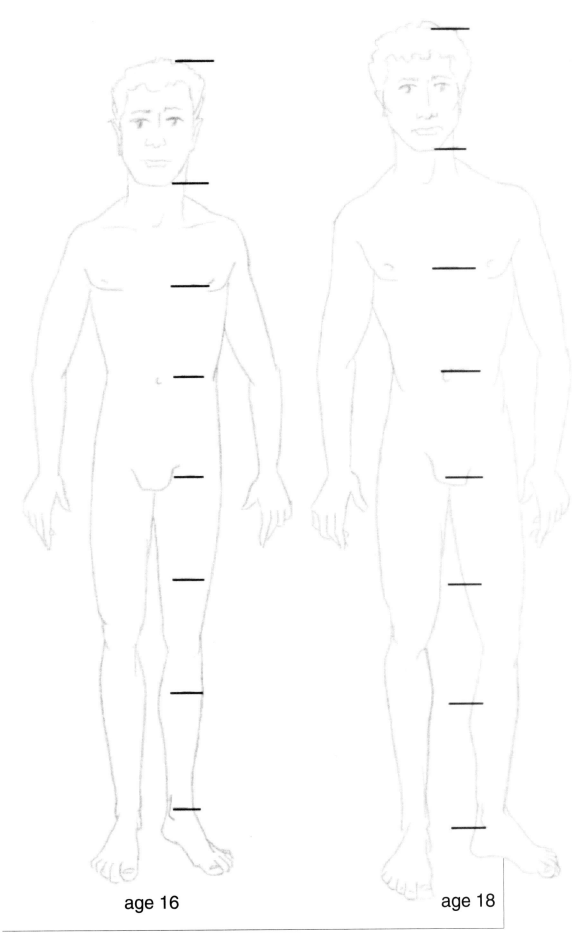

age 16   age 18

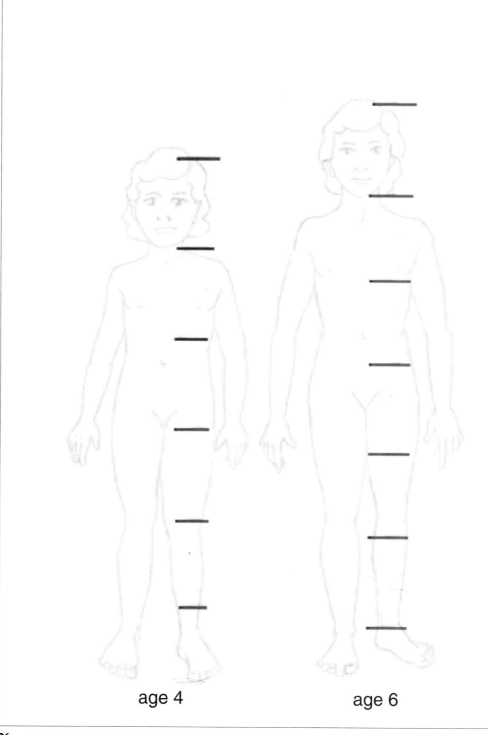

age 4

age 6

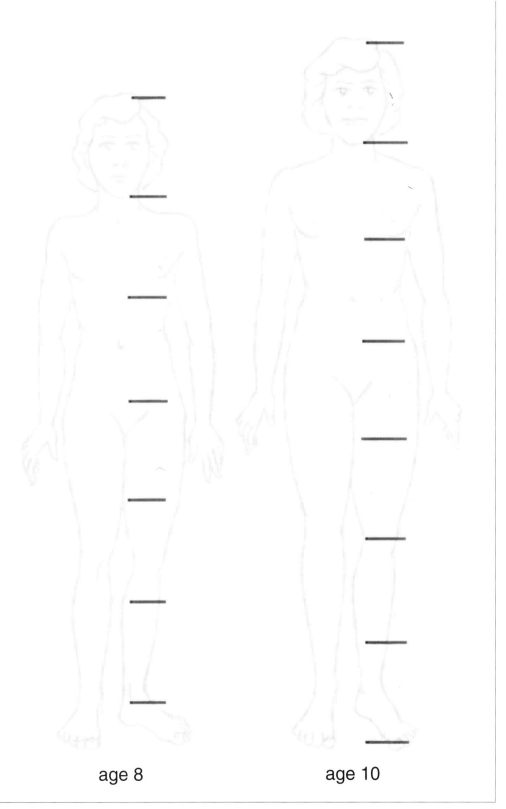

age 8   age 10

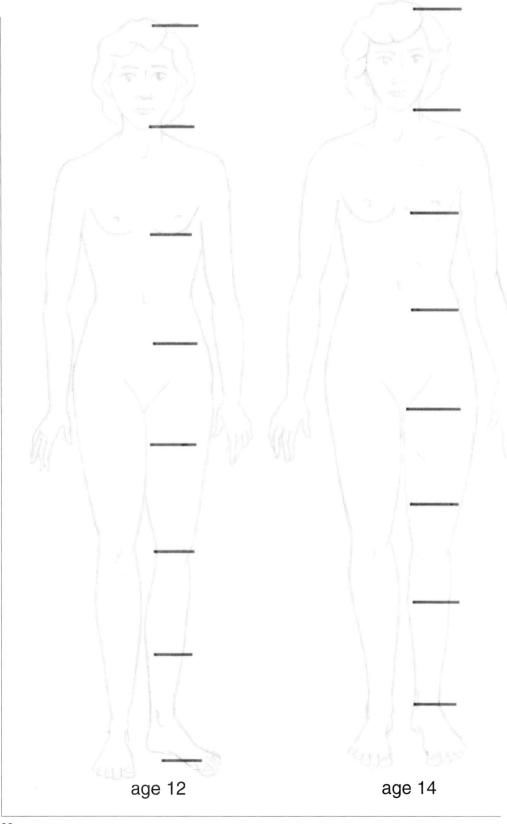

age 12   age 14

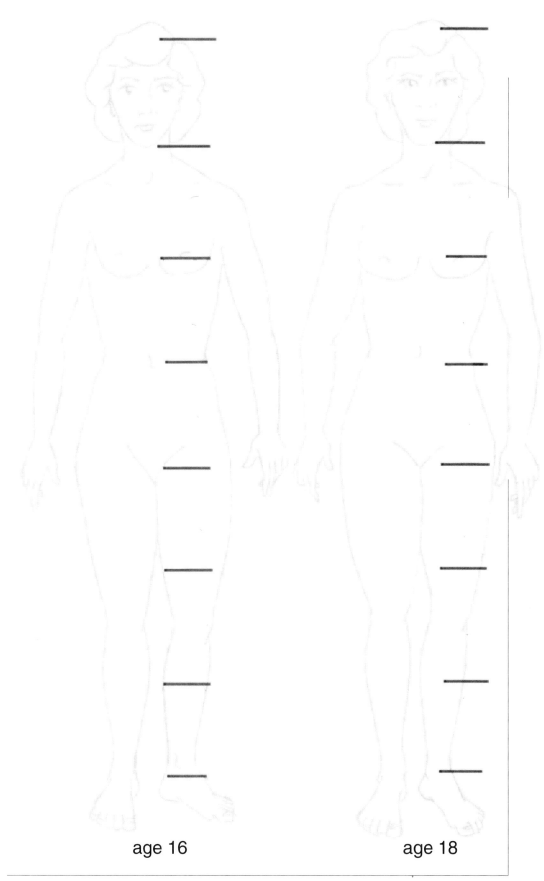

age 16   age 18

Even within the world of adults the 7$\frac{1}{2}$ Heads measurement system only allows for average body proportions. Simply lengthening and shortening standard proportions when necessary will make some difference in the figures created. However, body weight has the greatest influence on the overall look of the human form. Thin people seem to be taller and heavy people seem to be shorter. The true difference lies in the ratio of widths to lengths. Let us look at how we can apply different weight ratios to our figures.

Here is a proportional figure from one of our previous exercises.

And here is the figure completed in a "thin" ratio. Note that the only change is the actual body drawing technique used over the proportional doll. By staying close to the skeletal shapes of the human form and removing most of the muscular tissue, we have created a thin physique. Of course, this means more personal study of actual thin body shapes but the technique itself is simple in approach.

Adding body weight is a bit more challenging. As the body accumulates fat cells, it stores them in different areas of mass. To complete a heavy physique we need to add mass over the proportional doll *before* we draw the finished body.

Here is the proportional figure as before.

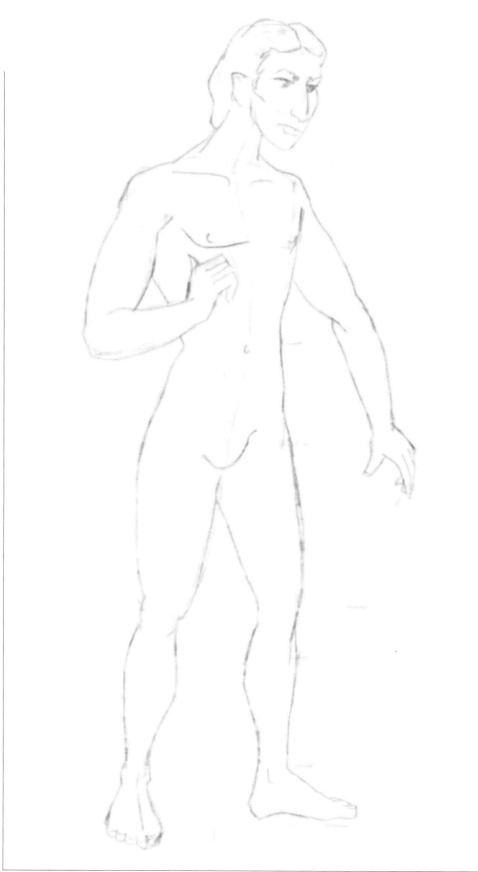

Since we will wind up with an overlapping abundance of these mass forms, we are smart to begin at the back and work towards the front of the body.

1. **We begin by adding "balls" of mass where fat cells tend to accumulate. Here we have used the Glass Technique to add the buttocks, calves, back waist and triceps.**

2. Here we have added mass to the sides of the body: hips, thighs, shoulders, neck and cheeks.

3. And now we finish with the front masses: throat, chest, arms, stomach, abdomen, and front thighs.

4. Now, with this new "doll" we can sketch over the proportional frame with added masses to create a heavy physique.

Again, this requires some study of actual obese body shapes so that placement of masses shows an understanding of true fat distribution.

Altering the proportional frame for different body physiques is not as complicated as it may seem, but it does require personal study of these varying body types. Use visual sources from books or magazines to add traced studies to your Body Morgue. These body shapes may be harder to find but their addition to your Body Morgue will provide valuable future resources for character drawings.

OTHER APPROACHES TO FIGURE DRAWING

5

Before we leave figure drawing, we will look at other drawing techniques for capturing the human form.

Our first exercise will reflect the dimensional body structures we touched upon in the last segment as we looked at joint movement. Approaching body movement with block figures can help the student understand the hinge mechanisms of the human body.

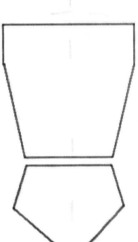

1. We will begin by drawing the oval for the head and marking the Head lengths and widths as before.

2. Within the length markings we now draw in the basic body blocks. Different shapes are used to represent the inflexible structures of the body. Here we have sketched in the torso and hip area. Note that the torso block is a reversed triangle whose points have been cut off at each joint (the waist and the two shoulder sockets.) Likewise, the hip block is a triangle with points cut off at the crotch and hip joints.

3. The rounded joints are drawn in. With this system each joint overlaps the blocks enough for attachment purposes. We also draw the neck and the shoulder curve.

4. A Plummet Line is drawn in to help balance the figure.

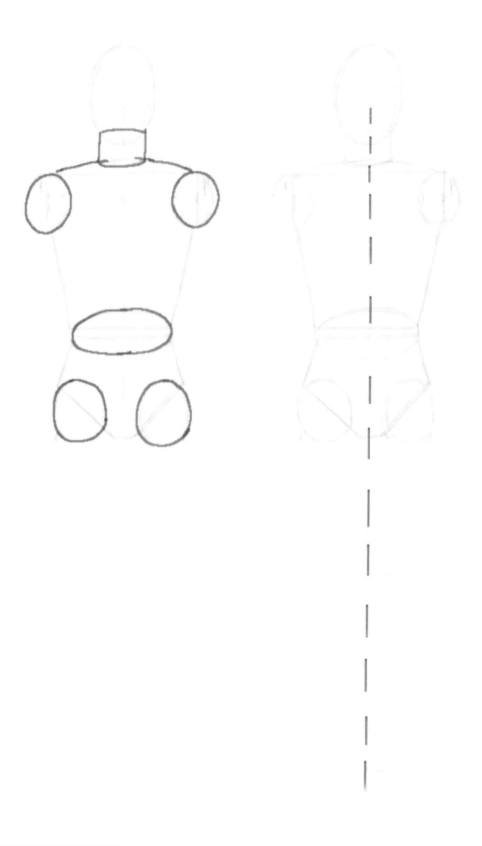

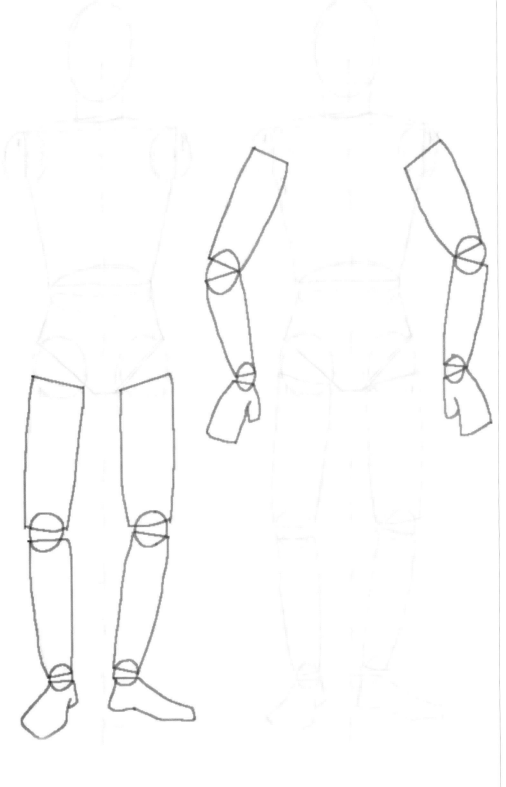

5. **From the hip joints, the blocks of the upper legs are sketched in. Knee joints are added. Lower legs, ankles and feet are also attached. We have done all this in one step since it is so closely re-lated to the process we have already used. Note that the same rules of gravity are employed, keeping the Plummet Line between the inside ankles.**

6. **Arms are added as in our previous exercises, using the shoulder joint, measuring lengths and employing an elbow and wrist joint.**

We now have a completed form that is very much like the figure we had before, but with structural reminders of the body regions. Even more than the previous steps we followed, this technique produces a drawing that is very reminiscent of the wooden manne-quin used by studio artists. We will be using our block figure in much the same way to create the final stance.

1. **We will back up to the step in the Head lengths have been marked and the torso and hip blocks have been added with the joints. At this point we can rotate the blocks on the rounded joints. Remember that, much like the wooden mannequin, the limited range of movement is expressed when two blocks rotate *into* one another, stopping the rotation. Here we have rotated the torso and hip blocks until we have been forced to stop.**

   To compensate for this contortion, note how the neck has also rotated with the blocks to keep the head vertical.

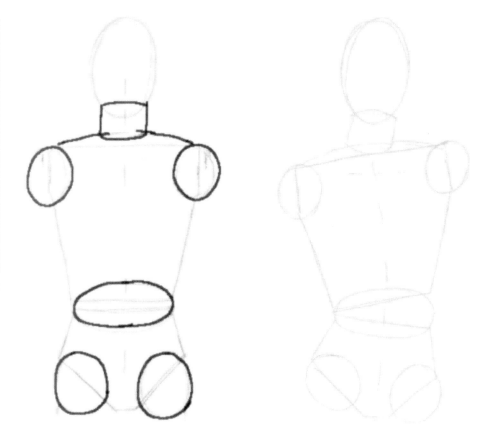

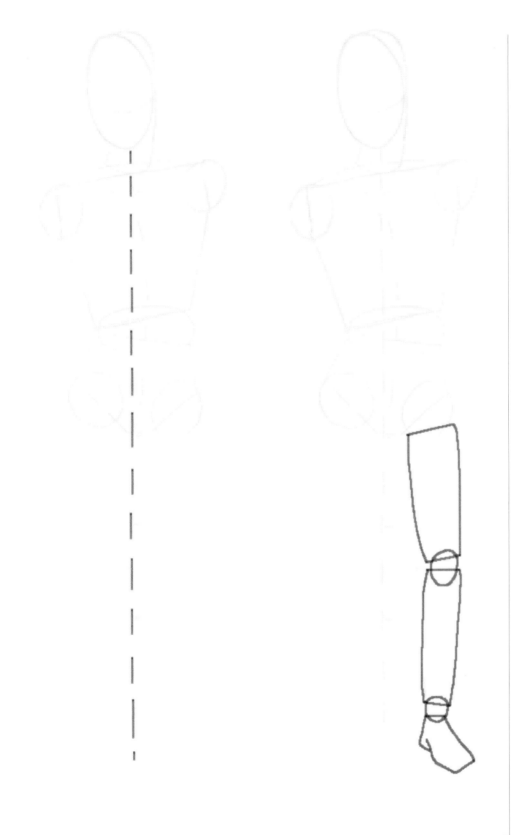

2. We draw in the Plummet Line. Note that we have also turned the head a bit for character expression, but this is only a personal choice.

3. We now add the legs. Beginning with the hip joint closest to the floor we can sketch in the leg segments. We will keep the Plummet Line close to the inside ankle of this leg to allow the other leg more freedom of movement.

4. **The second leg is sketched in using the measurements of the first leg to keep each segment the same length.**

5. **Arms are added.**

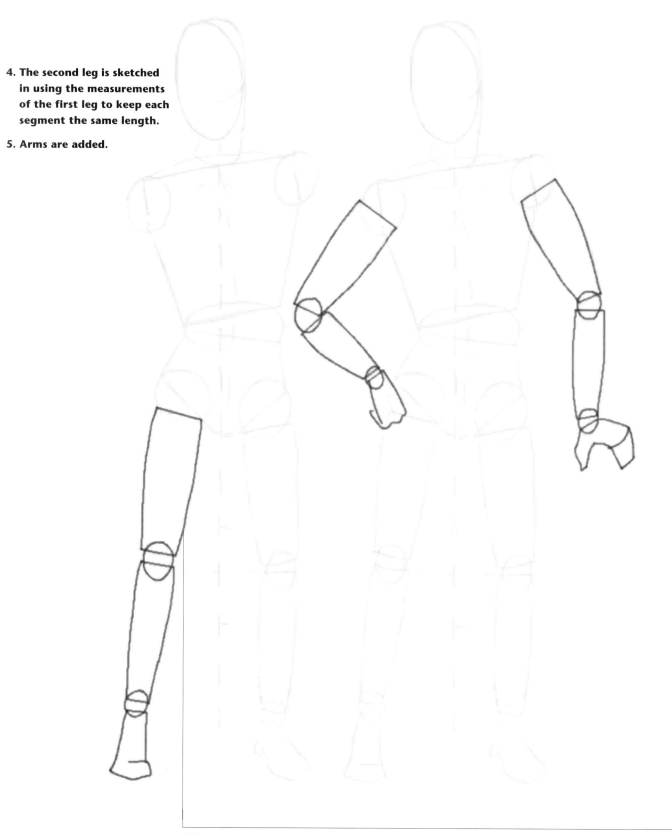

6. Skin is drawn over the block figure we created.

Study the completed figure and note the body angles that this method creates. There is a static, modeled effect to this technique that produces a less fluid shape in the final figure. Fashion designers tend to use this technique almost exclusively to produce figures less theatrical and more posed.

Here are some more figures
created using the block method.

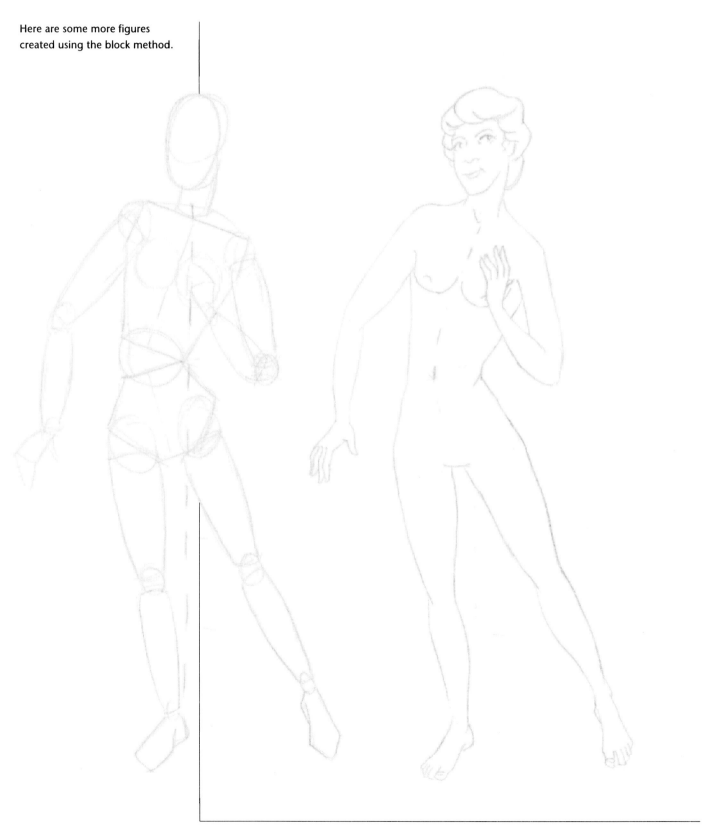

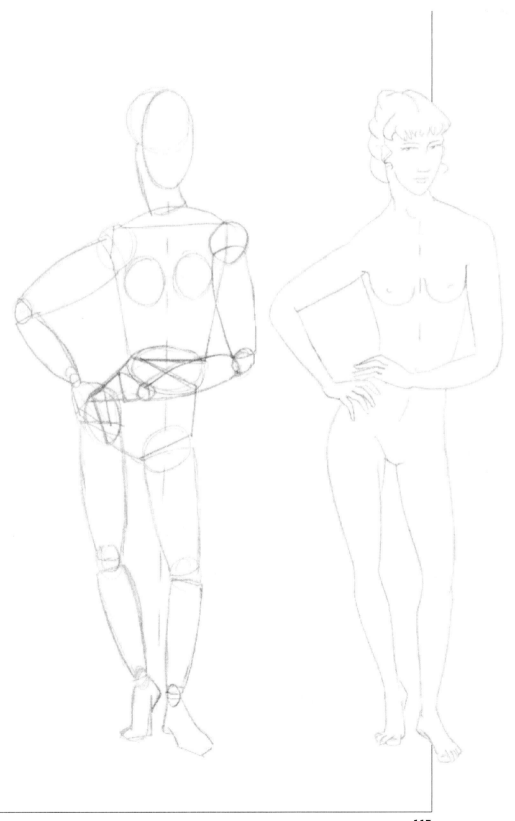

Fashion designers also tend to elongate the human form to make a taller, more slender figure. This is more attractive in showing the tailored lines of fashion clothing pieces.

Look at this elongated figure to see the technique of the fashion figure in use. Note that extra Head lengths have been added in the torso and leg regions. While these figures are attractive to the eye on paper, there is an inherent problem in their use by costume designers. Simply put, the finished costume will never look like the rendering. Elongation allows such a design more detail within the vertical form but, when placed on the shortened human body, the proportions are lost or appear squashed.

Since the costume designer is interested in producing renderings as identical as possible to the finished product, proportion is extremely important. If the director sees finished costumes that are not identical to those rendered, major problems can arise.

As a general rule, we will use true human proportions so that we can manipulate the costume design for a two-dimensional balance on paper that can be matched on the three-dimensional human form.

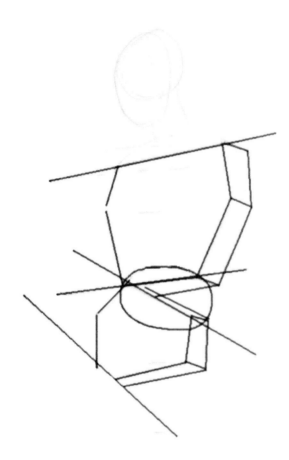

1. Now let us use the block method to create a three-quarters figure. The head is created with two ovals as before. The neck angle is added and the Head lengths are marked.

2. As the torso and hip blocks are placed, dimension is added to each. To accomplish the effect, some understanding of drawing block perspective is used. We will not go into this philosophy here, but the student who wishes to use this technique heavily should explore the rules of perspective thoroughly enough to produce forms true to perspective line.

3. The Center Front body line is found in this perspective view by drawing an "X" within the block shapes.

4. The center intersection of the two lines of the "X" mark the Center Front line, which is drawn in.

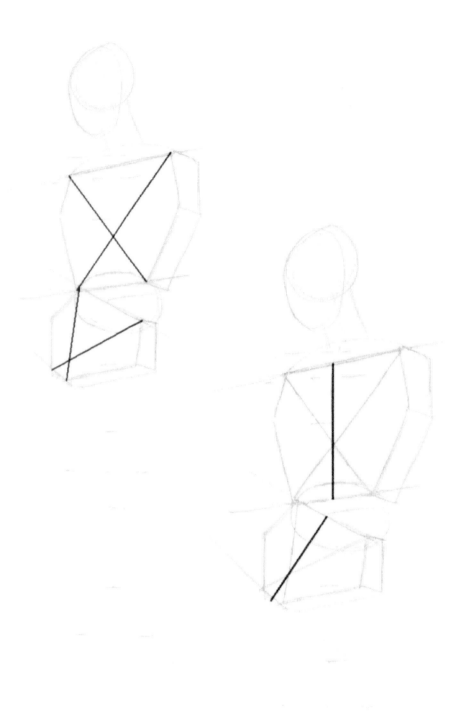

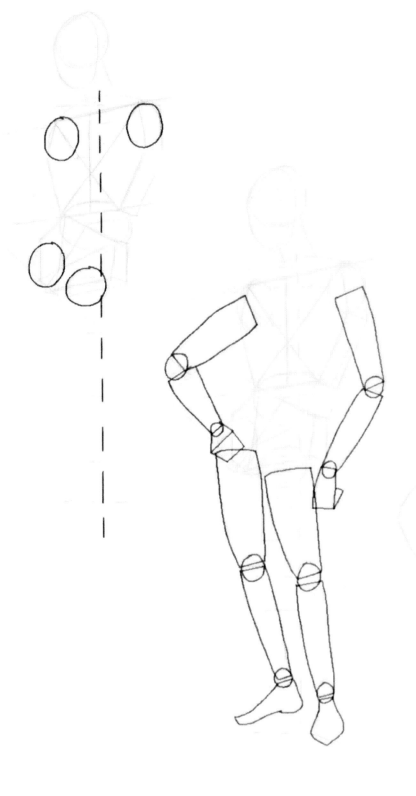

5. A Plummet Line
   is sketched in
   and joints are
   added using the
   Glass Technique.

6. Appendages are
   added.

7. The final form is
   completed.

Here are some more figures
created with the three-quarters
block technique.

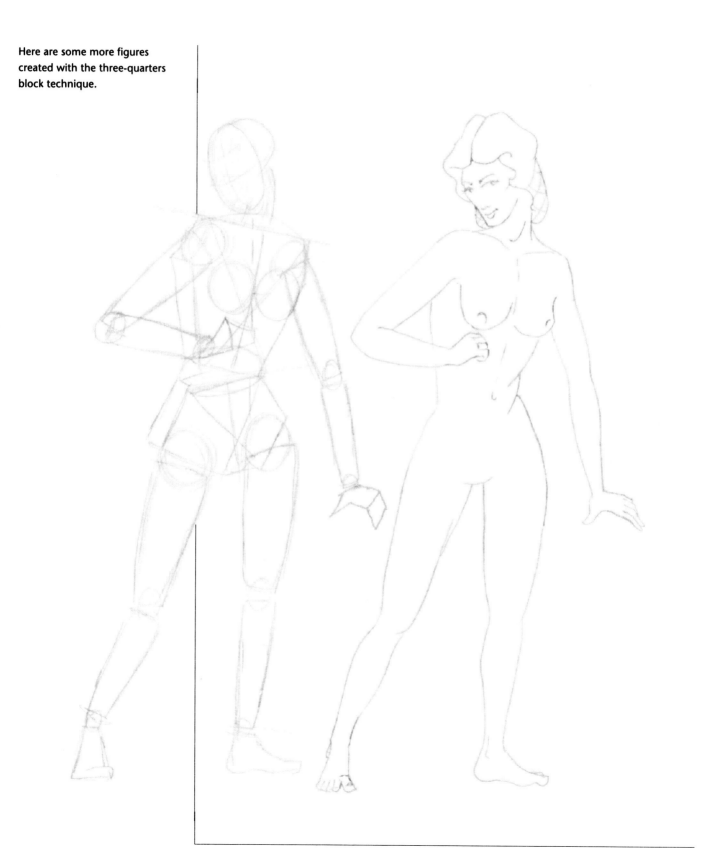

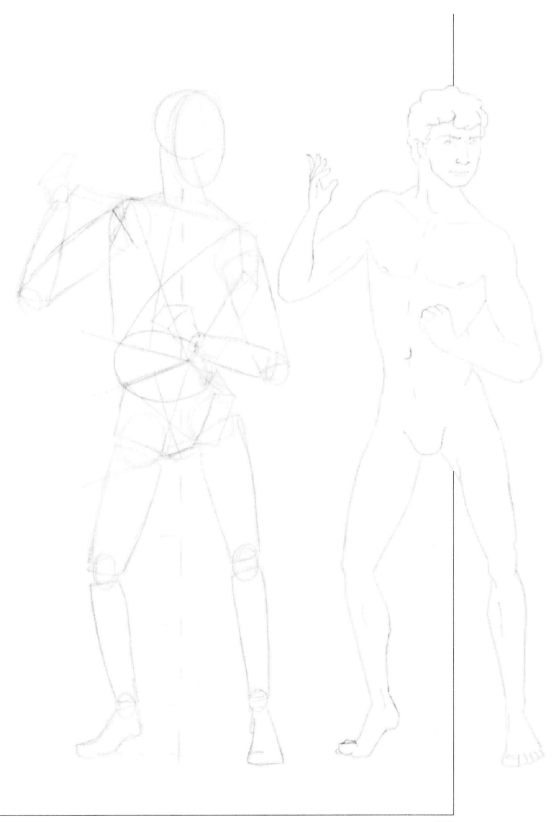

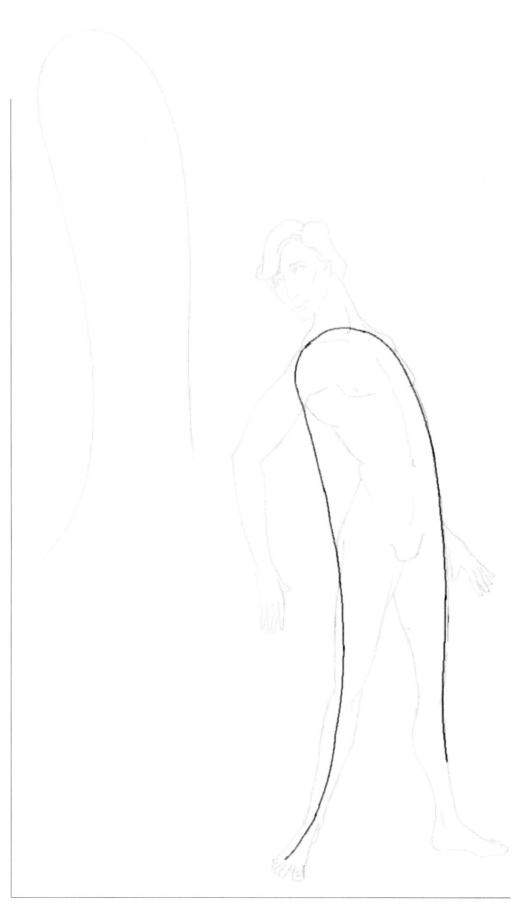

One last approach to figure drawing will help in creating figures with more free movement. In fact, the technique itself helps most students loosen the controlled lines of mechanical figure drawing and allows the mind to see the figure as a free-moving entity.

The proportional methods we have explored at this point often produce rather stiff figures. The method we will now investigate is especially applicable for producing figures for dance and other animated forms of theatre performance. It is known as the "loop method."

Before the student approaches this technique, he must have a good understanding of proportions. This method simply supplies outlines for figures within which the pro-portional steps are applied.

Begin with your hand and arm completely free from any support on the drawing surface. You will need the ability to create quick free forms in one swoop of the drawing hand.

1. In one complete motion, draw a loop on the page. A line of this nature lacks the studied positioning we have explored up to this point and creates a feeling of movement otherwise hard to capture. Now if we superimpose a figure on this loop, we can envision a moveable human form.

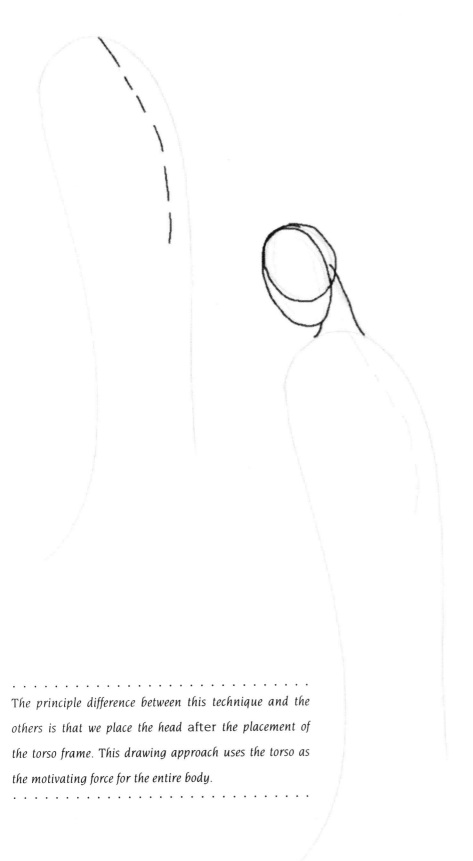

2. **Now, let us go back to the original loop. Looking at the shape of the curved line, create a Center Front body line to cut the loop into a torso. Note that we have *not* tried to force Head lengths onto the free form. We must trust our understanding of those proportions at this point.**

3. **Attach a head oval and neck, using the Center Front line to help guide placement.**

. . . .

The principle difference between this technique and the others is that we place the head after the placement of the torso frame. This drawing approach uses the torso as the motivating force for the entire body.

. . . .

. . . .

Try to create a figure within the proportions suggested by the loop itself. Of course, some loops may not produce a proportion as true as the previous techniques but this drawing method has much more to do with expression of form rather than hard-nosed proportions. But doesn't this contradict all we have disciplined ourselves with up to this point? Exactly! We do not want to create figures that seem mechanical and stiff. Learning the proportional steps was important, but now we need to learn to see proportion and allow it to influence and not dominate our drawings.

. . . .

4. **With the head in place, sketch in the torso and hip regions, using whichever technique you prefer. Trust your new sense of proportion as much as possible. Remember, this is supposed to be a "freeing" technique. Let yourself go!**

5. Place the hip and shoulder joints using the Glass Technique.

6. Work in the legs, using the loop lines as a guide. Perhaps the balance will be a little off and some correction may be needed, or not. Remember, these figures are in motion and that means gravity can be abandoned to some degree.

7. **Finish the sketch by adding arms. Here the designer will need a little understanding of arms in the balance of the figure. How do arms work in relationship to the legs? You will learn best by doing; let us go back to the mirror. Force your own body into some of these "loop" positions and you will find it hard to leave the arms dangling at the side of the body. They will usually extend into positions to balance the placement of the legs. Study relationships. Learn from the living form.**

8. **Complete the figure by drawing skin over the skeletal form.**

Here are more loop figures
as examples.

. . . .

This figure drawing approach produces active forms with energy and creative proportions. Try a few on your own. You may find it even more interesting to play some music while you work with this technique. There is a flow to music that helps the hand and arm "dance" in the loop method.

For every show I design, I enjoy researching music to play during the drawing process. Each historical period has a rhythm of its own that is represented in all the costuming research. These rhythms become more apparent through the period's music. I try as much as possible to design from within the period, not from the outside looking in. This may require some research in areas not generally applicable to the costume designer, some reading may be necessary. I even like to research the period just prior and just after the specific period in which we have set the production. Understanding the flow of fashion, architecture, music and the whole "world" of the play helps greatly in making decisions for each of the characters, especially in finding fads or styles that each character might have embraced. I am always looking for some "hook" on which to hang the personality of each character in the play.

. . . .

With all of these figure drawing approaches behind you, hopefully you will see that the creation of the nude figure is one of the most important steps to the costume design process. Nice clothing and good painting techniques will never compensate for a poorly drawn figure. Costume design is the art of character interpretation. Capturing the individual personality for each moment of the play is crucial in supporting the visual development of characters within the show. Naturally the clothing pieces chosen and the color combinations used will play a great deal in that final effect. But the costume rendering you produce must do much more than capture a tailored line for the costume shop. The rendering must reflect character, mood, need for detail, and even emphasis of particular forms; a wide "language" of visual interpretations for each member of the production team who will use the rendering in his or her own particular area.

Practice. Understand the human figure. After all, it is your canvas on which to present your final product. Think of the rendering as a *means* to the final costume design. It is *not* the costume design itself but it *is* your most important tool for communicating a vision of the completed design.

The way in which you communicate on paper becomes vital to your finished product. Be professional from the beginning. Produce figures that are expressive of your interpretation and that of your production team. But, first and foremost, produce figures true to the nature of your own professionalism. Don't settle for *almost*. Draw, draw and then draw some more! The pencil is your most vital communicative tool. Find the best ways to use it!

APPROACHES TO CLOTHING THE NUDE

Before attempting to clothe a figure, remember that a nude improperly proportioned or positioned will never improve by trying to cover it up with a costume. Make sure the nude is accurate and the clothing process will become much easier. Period research is vital to any costume design. You as the designer need to first surround yourself with enough research to "feel" the period. Try to understand the basic shapes the people wore and research their customs and traditions as much as possible to understand why they wore what they did. Usually researching the period before and after helps immensely to see the progression of shapes for a particular period.

The most vital thing you must remember is that to the people of the period these costumes were clothing and not simply articles they put on for exhibition. Design with clothing in mind. Remember why you wear clothes and apply that human reasoning to each character. It is often better to envision a "wardrobe" for each character and then decide what he or she would wear on a particular day, much as you dress yourself each morning. Don't forget to allow the characters to be real: to eat, to sit, to be human. In other words, allow them to live as people and not merely exist as characters on a stage. The true reality of a costume is that it came from somewhere and is going somewhere. This makes us feel the world of the play existed before the play began and will continue after, creating a continuity for the production.

So while we create costumes to appear correct on the theatrical stage, they must also fulfill the reality of clothing choices for each personality within the real world of the play.

With the research before you and the constant reminder that these characters are people too, let us discuss some basic ideas in clothing the human figure.

The general outline of any form is referred to as the silhouette. The human body itself has a silhouette we would recognize instantly. Most clothing pieces change that basic silhouette somewhat, and indeed some periods of fashion change the silhouette dramatically. Whenever we add clothing we change the silhouette of the figure, much the way we changed the dimension of the skull by adding hair. We can not, therefore, use the figure's nude lines as clothing lines unless we are clothing it in a skin-tight leotard. Even then the costume will tend to pull and push soft areas of the figure and bridge gaps inherent in the nude form. Compare this nude silhouette with the figure wearing a leotard for an idea of how much difference even a simple, skin-tight garment can make.

A costume has to work at two levels within any production. First, it must be correct for the individual character at any given time in that character's progression. But, on a second level, the costume has to look correct in combination with the other costumes on stage. This we refer to as the "tableau," or the overall look of a scene at any one moment. In this regard the costume helps the audience see relationships between characters, find the principal character of the scene and understand something of the world in which these characters live. This demands much from the costume designer, for in this sense the costume not only relates to character but also to the overall meaning of the production.

As an example of how clothing alters silhouette, let us consider a male figure in a basic three piece suit. Note how each layer adds consecutively more dimension to the original human form.

1. This illustration shows our male figure with shirt and pants added. Note that as we clothe the figure it is important to leave the Center Front line as a reference for aligning clothing pieces. The buttons of the shirt will follow this Center Front line and curve with the natural shape of the torso. Note that the shirt adds dimension wherever the fabric is layered or fullness has been eased in (i.e. the cuffs, at the waist, the collar, etc.)

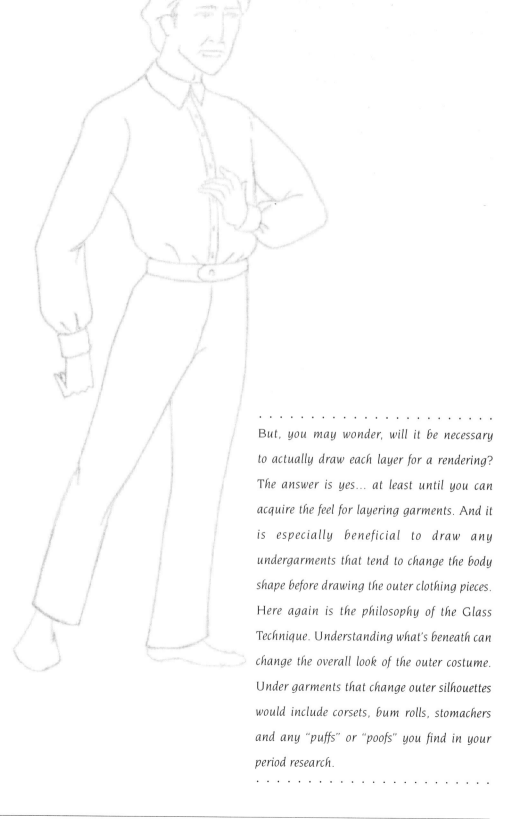

But, you may wonder, will it be necessary to actually draw each layer for a rendering? The answer is yes... at least until you can acquire the feel for layering garments. And it is especially beneficial to draw any undergarments that tend to change the body shape before drawing the outer clothing pieces. Here again is the philosophy of the Glass Technique. Understanding what's beneath can change the overall look of the outer costume. Under garments that change outer silhouettes would include corsets, bum rolls, stomachers and any "puffs" or "poofs" you find in your period research.

It may be wise to note that in the initial figure and under structure drawing process it is better to use a hard lead pencil (such as a 2H or 3H lead.) This makes lighter lines that are much easier to erase. Then, as you add the outer clothing, a soft lead pencil (such as an HB to 2B lead) can be used to complete the lines of the finished sketch.

The Glass Technique comes into play again as we create hems, collars and any other curved areas that encircle the body. Note that the cuffs are two ovals encompassing the wrist and that the collar is also an oval that wraps around the neck. The back of the oval is easily erased once we have found the correct position.

The pants add more dimension to the lower part of the body. The hems of the pants are created with the Glass Technique as well. Note also that because gravity affects the hang, the pant legs pull in toward the gravity line of the body. We have lost the muscular curves of the arms and legs now as the fabric has "bridged the gap" for us. As you sketch in clothing, an eraser can be used to remove the body lines beneath.

2. **Here we add a vest and tie. They both follow the center front line. The vest tends to pull much of the shirt back into the shape of the torso but we cannot use the original figure silhouette because the fabric weight adds some dimension. Note the amount of dimension we have added in the areas where fabric wraps around the edges of our figure.**

3. Now we sketch in a jacket. This adds more to the dimension of the silhouette, due to the padding and inner lining of a tailored suit. Shoulder pads raise and somewhat extent the shoulders, the roll collar fills in the neck curve and the shaping of the suit itself will alter the look of the torso greatly. Arms also become less muscular and are now more "tube-like."

4. This is the completed three piece suit with all internal and "glass" lines removed. We have kept the original figure's overall character stance and have wrapped the clothing around the form, using the Glass Technique.

As an exercise, let us create a female figure and clothe it in mid-1700s fashion, using a corset, bum roll and petticoat. Here is the figure we will start with, drawn in stance for the period.

1. **Let us first apply a corset. Note that the corset can only pinch in the silhouette of the female body where the body has no bone structure to resist. This area falls naturally at the waist line between the ribcage and the high hip. We must be careful not to exaggerate this alteration as most stage actresses will not allow us to tighten more than a couple of inches in the finished costume. If we cheat ourselves on paper we will create a look we will never be able to capture on stage.**

Note also what the corset tends to do to the bust line as it raises and rounds the breasts. Under structure research is just as important as outer structure research. Even if it doesn't show in the finished costume, under clothing changes the finished silhouette. Note also that the corset, though designed to pull in, will also add some dimension to the torso because of its boned structure.

2. **Now we add a bum roll using the Glass Technique for proper placement.**

3. **Petticoats are drawn to round out the bum roll's sharp curves. Note however that a petticoat must cover the bum roll's original shape and each progressive petticoat will add more dimension to the silhouette. Note also how the Glass Technique is used to find the simple hem oval to follow for the draped folds of the petticoat.**

4. **With under clothing in place, the dress is sketched in, adding yet more dimension to the figure. Note the areas in which the Glass Technique is used again to find proper hang and continuation of line.**

5. **The figure is cleaned, removing all hidden lines for the final effect. By the addition of a period costume, a dramatic change in the original figure has taken place!**

CAPTURING HANG, DRAPE & FOLDS 7

One of the major problems in costume sketching is the ability to capture the look of different fabrics through hang, drape and fold. No book can significantly show you all you need to know without some work on your part with actual fabrics on actual forms. The more you handle real fabrics and practice drawing them on various forms, the more you will begin to understand the techniques we will discuss.

But first, we need to understand some basic philosophy as to how hang, drape and folds are created. Of course the major influence is gravity.

Fabric will always tend to follow the Plummet Line you used to balance the figure. This refers in part to the *hang* of the fabric. The actual resistance or willingness of a fabric to follow gravity's pull will become part of the full effect of hang. Just remember that, generally, fabric will "fall" with gravity no matter in what shape it is cut.

Drape refers to the way fabric reacts to the form on which it is placed. How it falls from the shoulder point, contours around the chest, maneuvers over the waist line and then drops to the hem line is drape.

Folds are created as a fabric attempts to wrap around a movable shape. The fabric is pulled or pushed in different directions, forcing it to contort from its original "flat" self and create "bunched" areas called folds.

. . . .

And while we are discussing fabric's flat nature, let us mention "memory." The term refers to a fabric's ability to return to its original shape... flat. When you stand up, do your pants remember to as well? If they tend to bag at the knee the fabric has lost its memory. Some fabrics (such as knits) have little memory and are meant to be form fitting (such as the Spandex used in dance wear.) Other fabrics need to have strong memory, such as those used in tailoring a suit. For a nice, tailored look fabric needs to lay flat immediately out of a curved seam line. Knits make poor suits and wools make even worse dance wear. It all has to do with memory.

. . . .

To begin, let us talk a little about the graphic representation of folds we will use. Look at this photo of an actual period costume and then the graphic representation next to it.

Note that not all of the folds are actually drawn. In fact, in graphic representation we are always better to have as few lines as possible. The reason for this lies in the very nature of graphic representation. We are not drawing reality, we are simulating it. The lines we draw on paper to represent the silhouette of the sleeve and the lines we draw within the sleeve itself to represent folds are, in reality, the same in weight, color and thickness. This is *not* true in real life. Folds are "lights and shadows" of a color and texture, while silhouette is a contrast between a shape and its background. They have inherent weights, colors and thicknesses difficult to define graphically. So, we must choose to represent them with artificially drawn lines.

And how do we do so? Well, study the photo and drawing we just discussed. There are some common elements from which we can learn. Note these two rules for folds: 1) *They come from some place* and 2) *they go some place.* They don't just appear and disappear on the garment surface. Rule 1 infers that they have to originate from a source, be it a seam line, a bent arm or an extended knee. The beginning of the fold we draw has to come from its source.

Rule 2 deals with a little understanding of fabric and the technique of graphic representation. Some folds will run into another seam, into a hem edge, or another ending point. Other folds will "spread out" into the fabric, dealing with the memory ability of fabric to relax back into it's original flat state. Look again at the graphic representation of the period dress. A technique used in drawing folds consists of a small curve at the end of the line. Look at the fold marked "A" in the photo. Then look at the graphic representation of this fold and see how a slight curve at the end of the fold line is used to represent its return to the flat fabric. Note also that the curve goes away from the fullness of the fold.

Now, let us discuss how folds are created in the first place. There are two types of folds: *pressure point* and *compression.*

When something pushes or pulls a fabric, a bulge is created, forcing the fabric to move from its original flat state. Look at this illustration. Elbows, knees, shoulders, breasts and other protruding shapes will push out on fabrics and create *pressure point* folds. Note that the folds tend to "radiate" from the area of the pressure point itself. Note, however, that these folds generally *do not* directly touch the pressure point itself but tend to begin an inch or so away, much like a dart in a clothing piece. The distance from the pressure point has much to do with the weight and the memory of the fabric. Again, working with actual fabrics is the best method for learning how different fabrics look in fold situations.

Look again at this graphic representation of folds. Some use the curve technique at both the beginning and end of the fold, thus showing a fold originating *and* ending within the middle of the fabric.

When movement of the body forces fabric to bunch up on itself, *compression* folds occur. They tend to bunch up most at the point where the highest quantity of fabric is compressed and will radiate out from that point of tension until they flatten back out into the original surface of the fabric. Look at these examples of compression folds in the illustration. Note again the use of the curve at the end of some of the fold lines. These two fold categories are often combined.

Here is an elbow bend, creating *compression* at the inside of the bend and *pressure point* at the elbow point itself. These folds radiate into each other but still begin from their originating tension point. Look back at the last two illustrations to find a combination of these two folds used in each.

Some folds are variations of these
two types. Look at this illustration
of a Greek himation. It is mainly a
combination of compression folds,
since so much fabric has been
draped around the body. But
notice how some pressure points
are created by legs and arms.

Now let us approach *drape*
and *fold* in specific fabric types.
Drape and fold will help distinguish
the fabric's inherent characteristics.
So the way we draw the fabric
will help the viewer interpret the
fabrication intended.

Silhouette again becomes a
major communicator as we approach
fabric illustration. The silhouette
lines will say much about the
weight, crispness and *texture* of the
fabric we are drawing. Let us look
at each of these three characteristics
of fabric separately as we practice
rendering them.

The *weight* of fabric deals with its thickness and fiber content. Generally speaking the more a fabric pulls *away* from the gravity Plummet Line, the lighter in weight it will appear to be. Heavier fabrics tend to "fall" more directly along the Plummet Line.

The *drape* of the fabric will also express its weight. Refer to the illustrations to see that the larger the flare in the hanging folds of these fabrics, the lighter the respective weight seems to be. Logic tells us that a heavy wool will not fly about in the wind as much as a light weight cotton. The flare of the fabric's silhouette conveys this in form.

Another area that will express weight in fabric is any compression fold region. The larger the roll of a compression fold, the heavier the fabric appears to be.

Note these illustrations using compression to show weight of fabric.

Crispness of a fabric refers to its range of stiffness or limpness, or in other words, its ability to bend. Most of the ideas we discussed in regards to weight apply also to crispness. Generally speaking the heavier the weave of a fabric, the higher its inherent crispness. The two characteristics seem to be highly related. However, it is possible to introduce crispness to lighter weight fabrics with the use of starches, paints or fabrication techniques (i.e. organza, chintz, netting, etc.) These fabrics can be distinguished by combinations of fold-rendering techniques. For example, netting will fight drape, giving us a broad flare in the hem line but it compresses very easily and gives us small compression folds.

Crispness will also show in the actual silhouette of the fold. We know general folds are rounded but as a crisp fabric fights inherent bend, the roll will become angular in shape. These illustrations show variations of crispness in fabrics. Note that the hem lines and the angles drawn in the internal fold lines show the crispness of the fabrics.

Our last trait, *texture,* is perhaps a bit more difficult to simulate on a flat piece of paper and it will appear a bit more artificial. Again, silhouette is a vital communicator. The outer edge of folds and hems can help communicate the degree of texture in the fabric surface. Study these illustrations for examples of fur, heavy wool, and sculptured pile fabric. Note also that internally added graphic lines also help in showing some textures.

To add to your Body Morgue, trace graphic examples of *hang, drape, folds, weight, crispness* and *texture.* You'll find some good examples in commercial pattern books where graphic techniques are used to demonstrate specific types of fabrics.

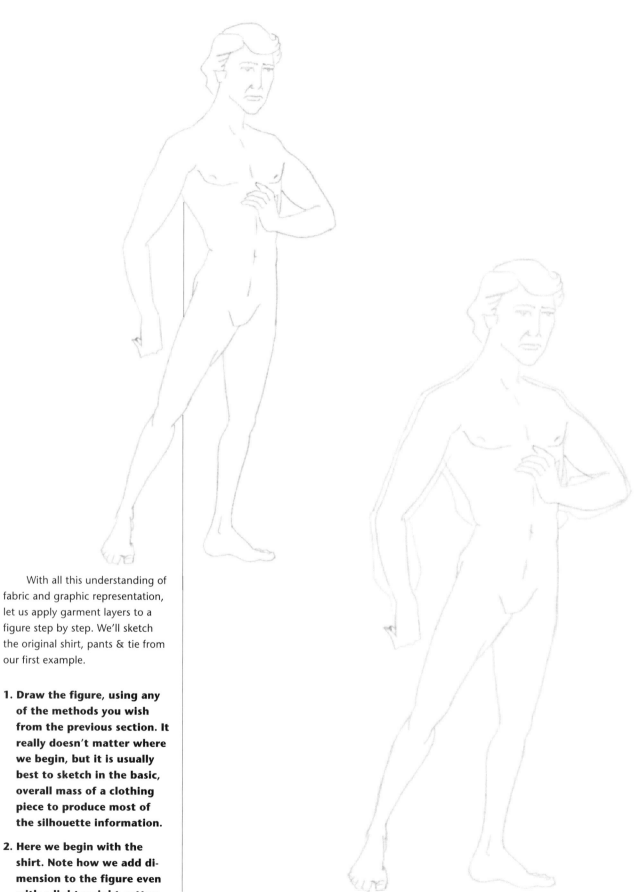

With all this understanding of fabric and graphic representation, let us apply garment layers to a figure step by step. We'll sketch the original shirt, pants & tie from our first example.

1. **Draw the figure, using any of the methods you wish from the previous section. It really doesn't matter where we begin, but it is usually best to sketch in the basic, overall mass of a clothing piece to produce most of the silhouette information.**

2. **Here we begin with the shirt. Note how we add dimension to the figure even with a light weight cotton fabric.**

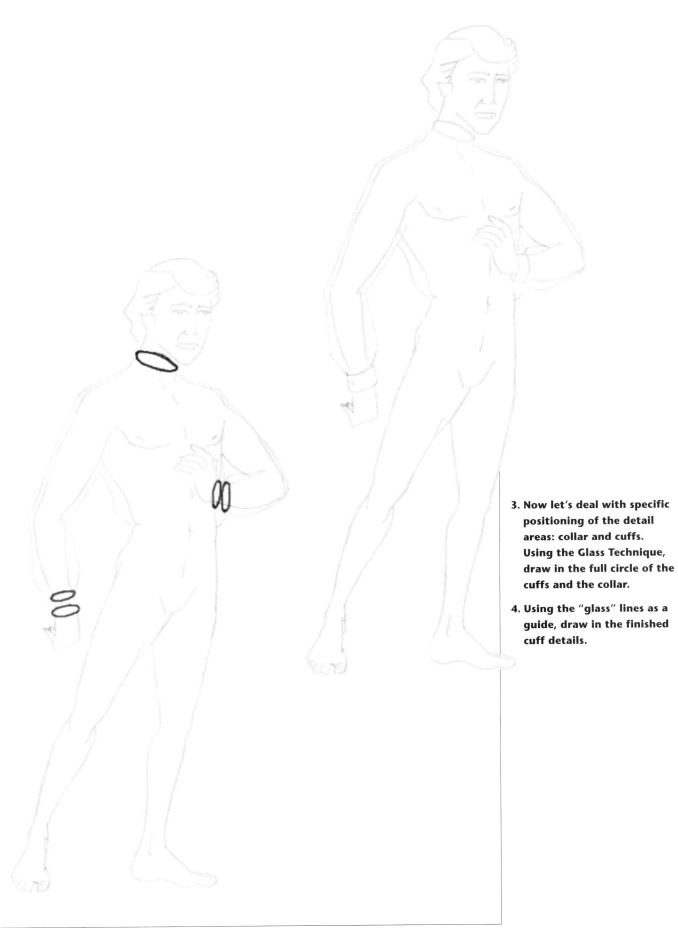

3. Now let's deal with specific positioning of the detail areas: collar and cuffs. Using the Glass Technique, draw in the full circle of the cuffs and the collar.

4. Using the "glass" lines as a guide, draw in the finished cuff details.

5. **We must follow two sets of guide lines for the collar: the oval "glass" line and the curved Center Front line. Draw in the collar shape, making sure to use the Center Front line to find true placement on the three-quarters figure.**

6. **Add the front placket for the shirt, following the Center Front line for placement.**

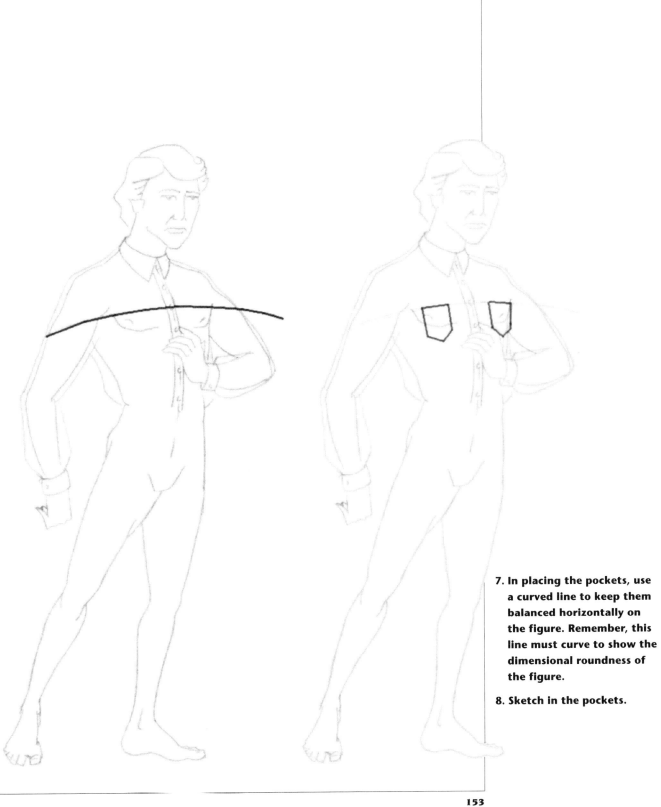

7. In placing the pockets, use a curved line to keep them balanced horizontally on the figure. Remember, this line must curve to show the dimensional roundness of the figure.

8. Sketch in the pockets.

9. "Tuck" the shirt into the pants by adding the top waistband oval using the Glass Technique. Represent the gathering of fabric by the use of compression fold lines. Note how a small curve at the outer end of each line shows fullness for each fold.

10. Clean up the sleeves, again showing compression in the cuff seam and the bunching of fabric in the bent elbow regions.

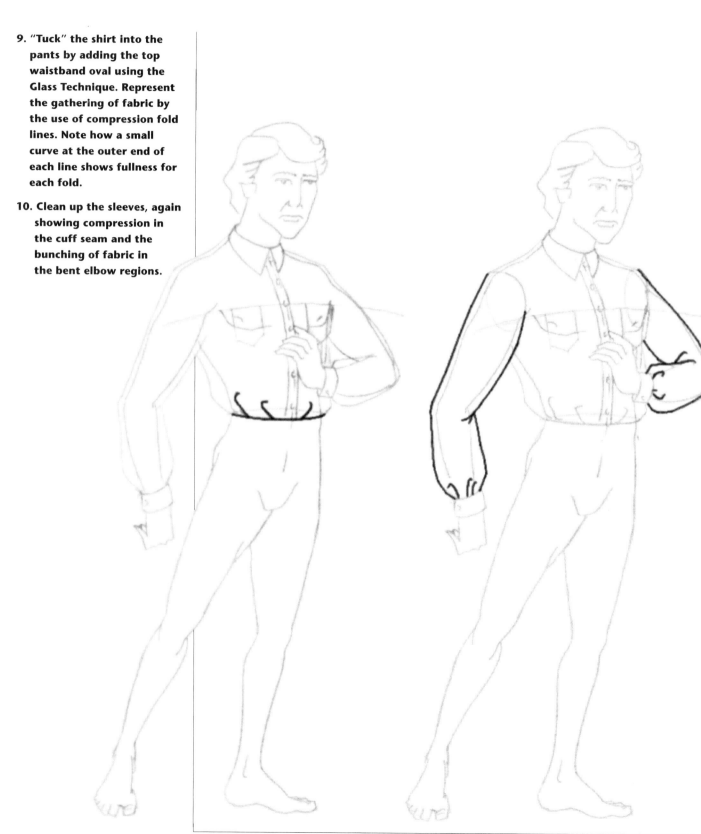

11. Draw the tie, using the Center Front line for placement.

12. Sketch in the second "glass" oval at the waist to place the waistband for the pants.

13. Now, show dimension in the hip region as you add the thickness of the waist band and the pants around the lower region.

14. As you drop the lines for the pant legs you must consider gravity. The pant legs will tend to swing towards the center of the body, trying to parallel the Plummet Line.

15. "Glass" ovals are added to place the cuff hem lines for each pant leg.

16. With all hidden lines removed, the figure is cleaned for the finished effect.

Work with these pencil techniques to establish the shape and the form of fabric. Practice clothing a few more figures on your own. Trace other drawings or photos if you want more help in these areas. Stay with contemporary clothing that does not greatly alter the original body shape at first. When you feel somewhat confident with simple clothing pieces, move on to more complicated period structures.

DEALING WITH BODY SHAPERS–HATS, SHOES & UNDER STRUCTURES 8

Approaching costume pieces that have their own artificial shape is much like approaching the original human figure. We need to literally build the costume piece using the skeletal shapes from which it is made. Some of the more common body shapers you will deal with are shoes and hats.

To learn the graphic lines for a basic shoe, let us enlarge the foot area so we can study shoe shapes. As we draw, keep in mind that the shoe will add dimension to the foot. We will simultaneously draw the foot from the side and from the front as we did before.

1. Here are the drawings we previously made of the foot. The typical shoe is made to fit the intricate curves and wrap tightly around the ankle.

2. **Start by sketching in the entire top oval of the shoe using the Glass Technique. Note that this oval is purposely curved to go under each ankle bone and pulls higher at the back to hug the Achilles tendon of the foot.**

3. **Now draw in the line of the heel of the shoe, noticing how it follows the natural extension of the heel bone. The shoe must curve up tightly to hug the tendon at the top of the heel or the shoe will slip in the walking process.**

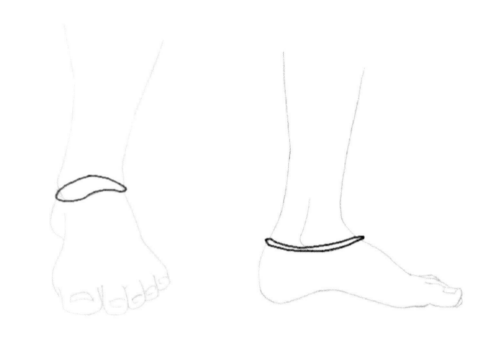

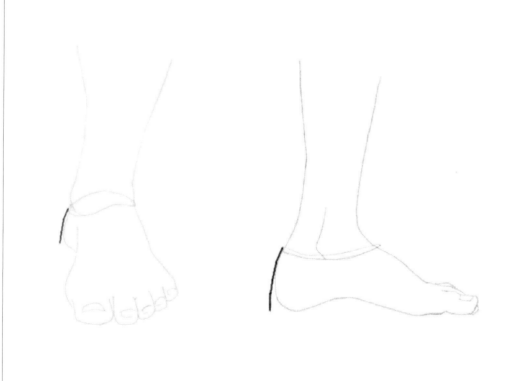

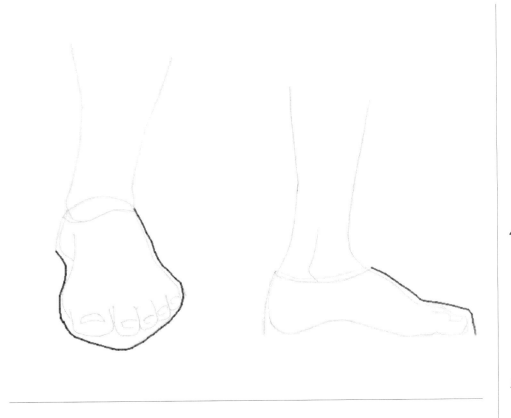

4. Add the toe of the shoe following the foot's shape. Remember to add dimension to the toe region. Note that the shoe points toward the second toe of the foot, which, as we already have learned, is the longest extension of the average foot.

5. The slit opening and tongue of a tie shoe follows the natural top arch of the foot and generally stops at the junction of the foot and the toes. These proportions have much to do with the design of the shoe you choose.

6. **Next we add the sole of the shoe. Note how the sole supports the natural arch of the foot with the heel added to raise the foot as part of that support.**

7. **Here is the finished shoe.**

There are hundreds of design variations but most shoes follow these basic principles of support and shaping.

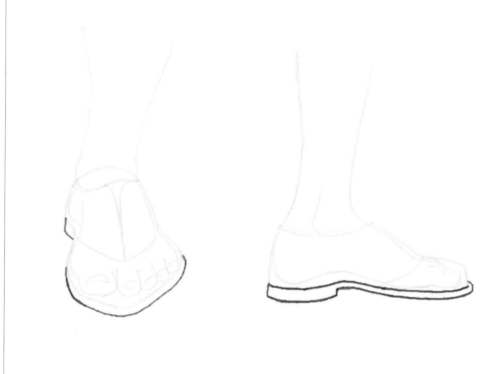

1. To sketch a shoe with a high heel, the foot must first be drawn in the correct position to stand in such a shoe.

2. At this point we follow the same steps as above, adding the oval for the mouth of the shoe.

3. **We add the back heel of the shoe.**

4. **Next, the toe is added.**

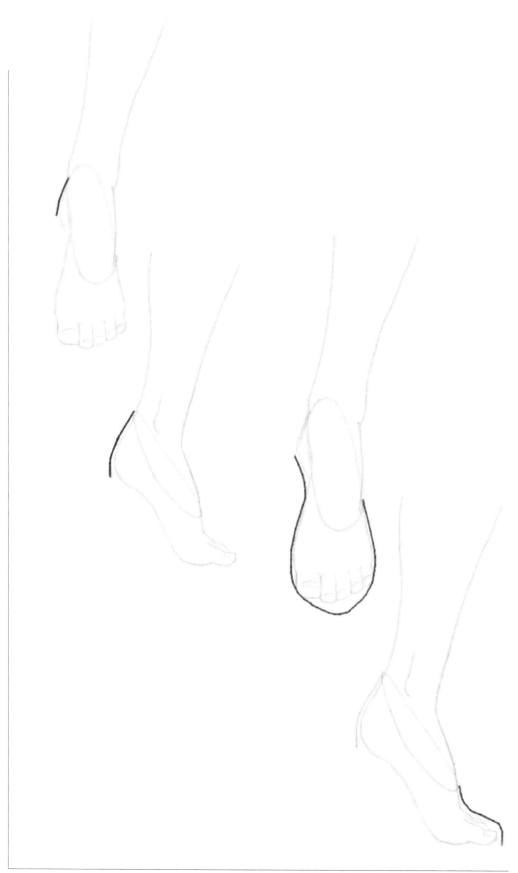

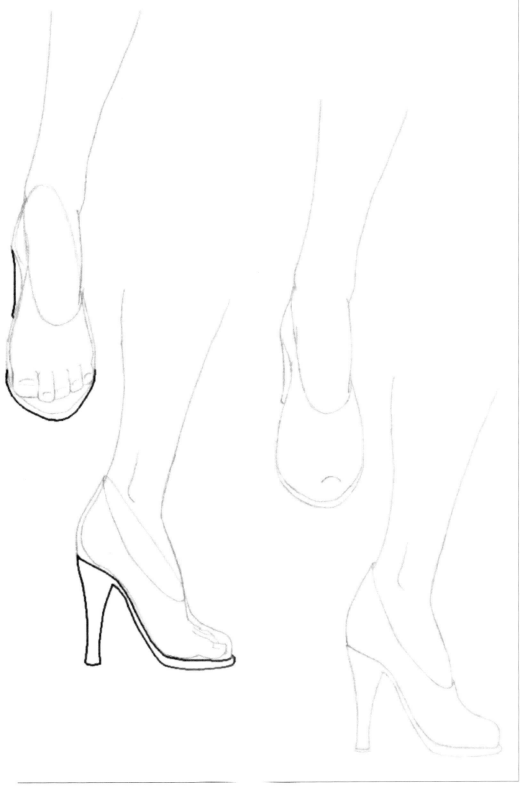

5. The sole is sketched in, with the high heel support itself.

6. Here is the finished shoe.

Practice a few shoes on your own. Use some resource pictures for different styles. Remember to draw the foot in the correct position *first* and then sketch the shoe *around* the foot.

Hats can be challenging to draw. They have their own skeletal system and generally do not attempt to shape themselves much to the skull itself other than the oval mouth that fits around the head.

Again, let us enlarge a human head for our study.

1. **With the head drawn, we establish the inside band placement where the hat fits the head. For this we use the Glass Technique. Note that this oval follows the original skull bone and compresses the hair closely to the head.**

2. **Now we create the crown attached to the hat band oval. Note that the top of the hat must be parallel with the original band oval and that the sides of the crown are roughly perpendicular to the horizontal plane of the hat band.**

3. We can shape the crown at this point for any particular fashion requirements.

4. To create the brim, we first draw another oval out and around the original band shape. We must realize that a brim is created from a flat oval whose outer edge is equally distanced out from the hat band. Of course some hats vary this distancing for effect and some have no brim at all, but this is the general technique. Again, we use the Glass Technique to create the complete oval for proper placement.

5. At this point we can shape the brim as needed in full "glass" fashion.

6. With the hidden lines removed, we now have a basic hat.

. . . .

Much time can and should be spent on practice in clothing the figure. Try several different periods with all their under structures. Be aware that some nude character positions will suddenly become cluttered up by period clothing, so you may have to redesign the nude before clothing it. Some fashions (such as the bustle) will not show up well in a front view. In these cases, the figure may have to be turned more fully to the side, or a full back view may even have to be rendered to more completely represent the construction of the costume. Sometimes additional sketches may have to accompany the rendering for construction information. Remember one of the most important purposes of your costume rendering is to communicate construction to the shop. With this in mind you may want to include some seam line information within the costume, just to help the cutter.

. . . .

7. We can add trim details to finish the hat design.

Here are a few more hat variations to try.

You will undoubtedly come upon other structures in your research that create new silhouettes for the figure. History is full of such pieces. Just remember to research their skeletal structure and then draw them on the body using the Glass Technique for correct placement. Just as we did with hats and shoes, build the structure out from the body, beginning with the portion of the structure that touches the body itself.

Here are a few historical costumes created as examples. Draw a few on your own. You may want to go to a costume shop and use some actual structures on a dress dummy to see how they proportionally fit the human body. Then study a little about the layers of clothing that go over them. Often these structures are only the beginning of many layers used to create the finished silhouette.

APPLYING PERIOD RESEARCH

As you begin to apply period research, you may find it difficult to correctly proportion a particular clothing piece. The art work of each period had its own look and most periods need to be adapted to contemporary human body shapes. I doubt that any actress would allow us to surgically remove her bottom rib as was necessary in the late 1800s to achieve the ideal nineteen-inch waistline! To complete such a look on stage, we must play with the relative masses within the costume to *force* the look of a nineteen-inch waistline instead. As we adapt period art in our renderings, we must frequently translate period proportions into contemporary proportions.

Here is an actual period costume we want to use in a production. The waist is an obvious problem, but there are other problems involved here as well.

Redrawn from "Harper's Bazaar," 11.1.1884, page 700

1. Start pinpointing the proportional problems by measuring the researched figure using its own proportional head.

This figure does not follow the same proportion rules we have implemented and if we alter our nude figure to agree with these period proportions, we will be doing ourselves an injustice. We can always make it look great on paper, but remember our costume will be worn by a contemporary body that follows the "seven and one half Heads" system we have studied. It is better to solve the problems on paper and predetermine how to adapt the period look.

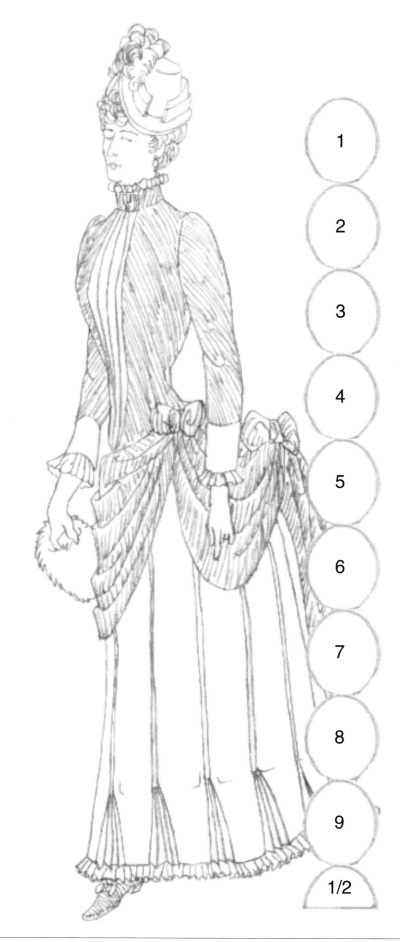

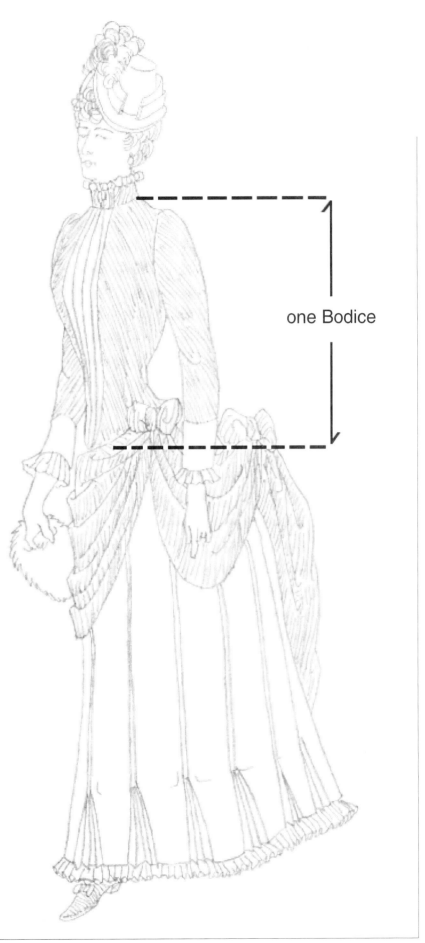

one Bodice

2. When we studied nude proportions, we used the Head as our constant measurement. To capture the proportions of a period costume we need to find a constant measurement within the period design itself. For this particular exercise, we will use the "Bodice." Measure out the period illustration and find out how many Bodices long the skirt is.

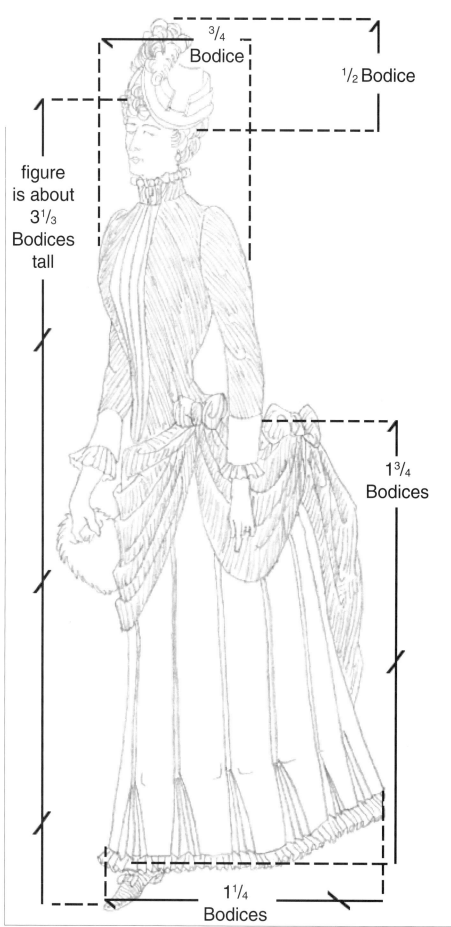

Measure the width from outer sleeve cap to outer sleeve cap. How many Bodices wide is it? How tall is the period hat? How wide is the skirt hem? And *most important,* how many Bodices tall is the figure itself?

3/4 Bodice

1/2 Bodice

figure is about 31/3 Bodices tall

13/4 Bodices

11/4 Bodices

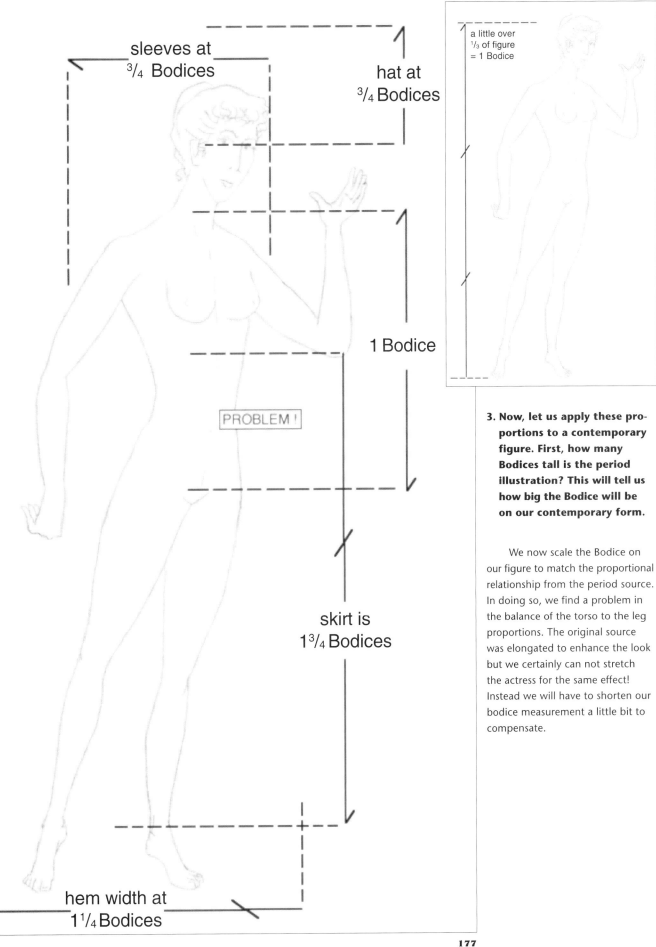

sleeves at
³/₄ Bodices

hat at
³/₄ Bodices

a little over
¹/₃ of figure
= 1 Bodice

1 Bodice

PROBLEM !

skirt is
1³/₄ Bodices

hem width at
1¹/₄ Bodices

3. Now, let us apply these proportions to a contemporary figure. First, how many Bodices tall is the period illustration? This will tell us how big the Bodice will be on our contemporary form.

We now scale the Bodice on our figure to match the proportional relationship from the period source. In doing so, we find a problem in the balance of the torso to the leg proportions. The original source was elongated to enhance the look but we certainly can not stretch the actress for the same effect! Instead we will have to shorten our bodice measurement a little bit to compensate.

4. **With the modified Bodice measurement in mind, sketch in the rough bodice and skirt. Make sure the length is in correct proportion (or Bodice lengths.) Also, check to see how many Bodices wide the hem of the skirt is and sketch it in correct proportion.**

5. **Add the sleeve caps using Bodice proportions. We are going to have to "cheat" the armscye seam in a bit on the shoulder to capture the period shoulder width.**

6. Sketch in the hat, watching the proportions in the period source.

We should now have the correct proportions but the waist will still be a problem. A corset will help but can not pull our contemporary form into the ideal nineteen-inch waist line of the period. Instead we will have to *increase* other width proportions to make the waist *appear* to be smaller.

7. Here we have increased the skirt flare, sleeve cap breadth and width of the front bodice opening just a little to create the narrow waist look.

8. We sketch in the rest of the costume detail using our newly increased silhouette. Note that the top skirt will help add some breadth in proportion to the waist size, so we use it wisely.

9. Clean up the drawing to see the finished effect. Now is a good time to adjust wherever we may need to fully capture the period proportions.

10. And as we add the values and textures of the original source, we find that the darker bodice only helps pull the eye into the thinner opening down the front, thus enhancing the slender look one more time. We have cheated the narrowness at the bottom of this opening, just to make the waist appear narrower. Compare the finished sketch to the original body and it will appear that the body has been reshaped, when only the costume was used to make the figure appear to be in period proportions.

Redrawn from "Hunter with Dog"
Vase by Pan Painter, 470–460 B.C.
(Original in Museum of Fine Arts, Boston)

Here are a few more sketches
showing period translations.

Variations on all of them are
possible, depending on the result
you as a designer want to achieve.
Study the original period sources
and compare them to the contemporary drawings. Note how costume
proportions were used to capture
the period look.

Try one or two period adapta-
tions as practice. Refer to these
period sources and see what you
can do to adapt the proportions for
one of your contemporary figures.

Redrawn from "The Visitation"
by Ghirlandaio, 1488–1493
(Santa Maria Novella, Florence, Italy)

Redrawn from "Journal des Dames
et des Modes," 1820
(Collection of Blanche Payne)

DESIGNING FROM THE NUDE

10

The nude figure has been created with the principles of stance and positioning, and you have enough research for a general command of the basic shapes and silhouettes of the period. You can now approach the costume design as an extension of the same principles you used for drawing the nude.

With a working knowledge of period shapes and choices, we are ready to clothe each character. We will use some of the Delsarte techniques we learned earlier.

. . . .

It is important to repeat the significance of period research at this point. Before you actually begin with costume shapes, an in-depth study of period costume pieces is essential. Research should include not only actual period visual findings but also written descriptions of how and why the people of the period wore what they did. I generally include research in the period before and after as well, just to more fully understand the evolution of fashion for the specific period. This allows me to determine where in this progression of fashion each of the characters should fall. When a specific year is chosen for a show, I consider that my "cutoff date." This simply means that no character will wear fashion influences after that year, but many may wear fashions from several years before. Much depends on character personality, age, and financial ability to keep up with the fashions. This is what character interpretation is all about. Many of these decisions should be made in close conference with the director, since major influences on character development are hereby imposed.

. . . .

1. Let us return to the male nude for Hamlet we created in Chapter 1. We should feel good about the figure itself, but there are a few character traits we still wish to enhance. We want Hamlet to appear vulnerable in the scene. The more the costume reveals the original body shape, the more vulnerable the character will appear. This does not necessarily demand that bare skin shows but merely that the natural body line be revealed. Also, the more layering of fabrics we use, the more he or she seems to be hiding.

Revealing original body silhouette is one of the keys
vulnerability for a character. Vulnerable characters seem mor
at risk in their environment. We are more personally concerne
about their decisions and we more easily relate to them. A
designers, we can add multiple layers of clothing on
character but as long as original body silhouette is not drasticall
altered, the character will remain vulnerable. As soon as we ad
any clothing pieces to mask silhouette (such as capes, cloaks, o
robes) we impede not only the character's movements but als
the audience's perception of the character's outward motivations

2. **It is advisable to begin in the torso region, since this area of "true conviction" shows character development more than any other region. We will choose an open neckline for Hamlet to expose his emotions. This could be an excellent way to reveal his struggle between duty and personal freedom.**

3. **We will also choose to keep Hamlet's lower region clean in silhouette up to the crotch line so that his sexual advances on Ophelia appear dangerously real. A period cod piece will further emphasize this region.**

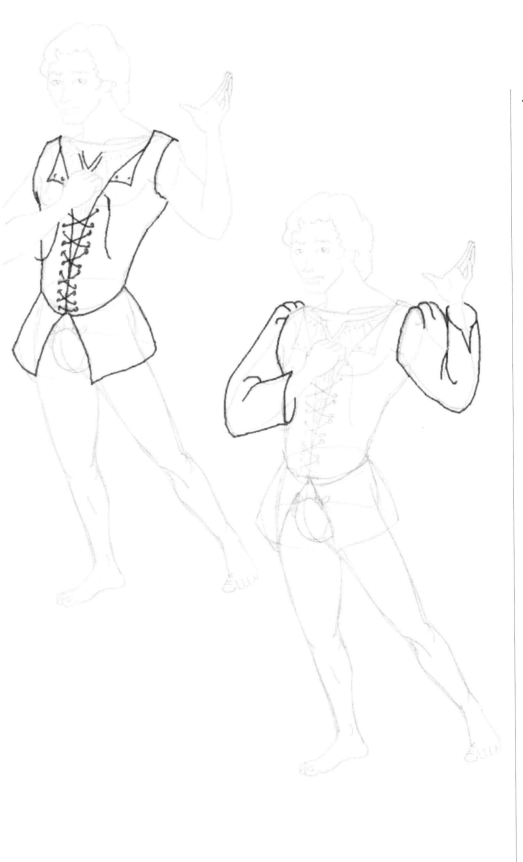

4. **By making sure the neckline itself is angular and not curved, we can create tension in the heart region.**

We also want to layer the heart region since Hamlet himself has difficulty discovering his own motives. We add a jerkin with an angled opening to reemphasize our statement. We also add a laced front, offering Hamlet the ability to open his heart region and remove his layers. Good costume design frequently offers possibilities for character development, whether or not the character chooses to use them.

5. **Above all, we want to show Hamlet's precarious position in the decisions he must make. He is torn between "head" and "heart" (the knowledge of what he *should* do and the dilemma of what he *feels* he should do). This conflict will emphasize the "middle ground" between these two regions: the shoulders. We choose a leg-of-mutton sleeve with a strong shoulder cap to strengthen the shoulders. This should help "divide" the head from the heart.**

6. It is probably best to keep Hamlet's head bare, as he should be "vulnerably head strong" as well. Hair style will become very important. If we add a mass of hair, we may obscure the region. But short hair is not quite period. Research may have to help our decision. We will chose a length somewhere in between.

Also, by adding some texture to the hair we can add detail emphasis to the region. This will offer conflict in philosophy and the possibility of intellectual change.

7. Shoe style will affect the base strength of the character. Compare a couple of choices. The pointed toe of the second shoe is probably too comical, so the first option is our best. This style offers some foundation for the character without pulling too much focus.

. . . .

Angle of line within a region is an important decision. Curves suggest less opposition, are more "feminine/emotional" by nature, and are often used for comic purposes. Angled lines, pointed cuts or "carved" details tend to present opposition, tension and conflict within a region. We can enhance such lines by choosing to double layer the region with repeating lines or by placing piping along the seam line to enhance the effect. Conflict within any region suggests to an audience further possible development in these traits. Make sure you say what you mean, and make sure the script offers support for your choices.

. . . .

. . . .

Detail adds depth. When we add detail to the head region, we offer thought process for a character. The audience becomes more interested in what the character thinks. If we add detail to the heart region, we add confusion or possibility of change in personal conviction for the character. Study the Delsarte regions once more and notice the ways a costume designer can use detail to offer possibility of change for a variety of human characteristics within the finished costume.

Lack of detail within a region professes conviction of a character. It offers little chance for change and, consequently, characters appear to have strong convictions that are less likely to alter in the course of the play.

Tight fitting clothing within a region adds restriction for the character. Open clothing adds release. Lacings, buttons or zippers offer the ability for the character to free themselves.

Placement of details, openings, restrictions, contrasts or any other design elements within Delsarte regions can be an effective way of visually offering character development possibilities to support the actor's work. A good costume can enhance an actor's performance in many ways.

. . . .

8. Here is the finished costume developed through the choices we made. As we created the costume for Hamlet we were aware of his strengths, vulnerabilities and actual weaknesses at this particular moment of the play.

. . . .

As we now present the design to the director for his or her reactions, we will know how to respond to comments such as, "He appears too open and too vulnerable," or "He doesn't appear to show enough strength in his convictions." We can adapt the design in specific regions to "add" or "take away" as needed.

. . . .

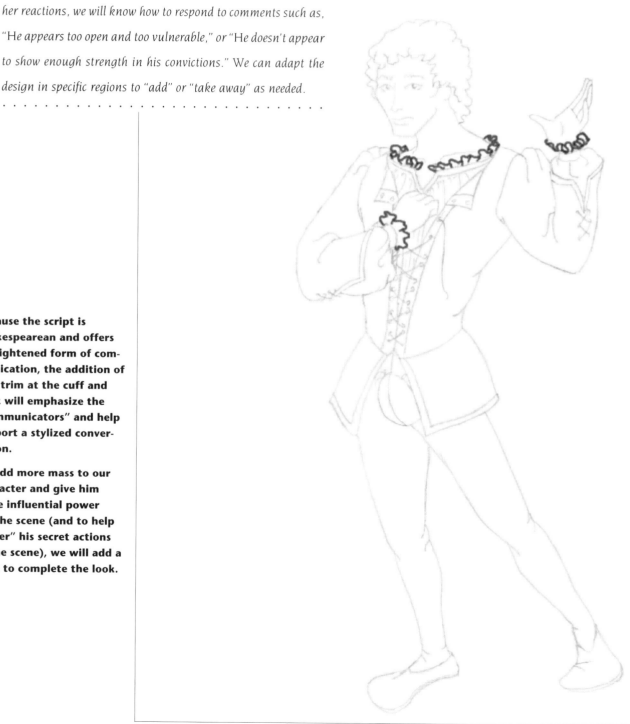

9. **Because the script is Shakespearean and offers a heightened form of communication, the addition of lace trim at the cuff and neck will emphasize the "communicators" and help support a stylized conversation.**

10. **To add more mass to our character and give him more influential power for the scene (and to help "cover" his secret actions in the scene), we will add a cape to complete the look.**

. . . .

It can be argued that much of our character expression is in the figure stance. How will the costume appear if the actor doesn't stand in this one position for the entire scene? Of course we have to rely on the actor's application of the costume for the full character development, but the costume was created out of the basic characteristics the actor will be using as long as we have had meaningful production meetings with the director and other staff members. There is no way we can draw a costumed figure in all the variations of stance that an actor will go through in just one minute of a scene. The techniques we have used for figure stance were merely a means of communicating our character analysis to the director, and the costume was a natural product of that analysis.

. . . .

Here are two more costume interpretations using the techniques we just explored:

1. **This is Anne Page from *The Merry Wives of Windsor* by William Shakespeare. We first note that she is facing the "wrong way" on the paper. This demonstrates a rebellious nature to her presentation. Next we note the chest emphasis with a strong horizontal line between the heart and sexual regions. This allows her to be open emotionally but not sexually to her young suitors. The added choice of a layered skirt gives us a bit of a peek into the more complicated layers of her sexual interests. The loose, rounded sleeves keep the heart area romantic and the sheer veil offers a somewhat transparent coverage for her intellect. Her hand "communicators" are somewhat stifled, showing her submission to the words of others who control her. Yet the soft lace at her breast allows what words she does emit to come forth in all their simple beauty.**

2. **And here is the character
Stinky from *Mrs. McThing* by
Mary Chase. This character
offers us a fairly typical
gangster look with a bit of
a comical twist. Though he
"flows" with the crowd
(right to left), note his hesitant glance in the wrong
direction. This offers a
"teasing" nature to his
point of view. His loose
clothing gives us not only
an unkempt feeling but an
almost naive edge to his
attitude. He seems to be
hiding something in the
heart region—perhaps his
loyalties? And the high
hems of the pants show a
weak, comical foundation
to his nature. This is balanced by the same "short
wit" in the heart region.
He seems to be just a softy
after all!**

. . . .

At this point, perhaps a side comment should be added. I
feel, as a designer, a certain responsibility to the actors at
this point of the design process. They are usually in the
early stages of production, and I feel an obligation to show
them character choices I have made for them. I have found
that a presentation of the approved costume designs to the
entire cast early in the process is vital to their own character
development. Why surprise them the week before they open
with what I have interpreted they should wear as the
character? I choose to let them see the designs as early as
possible so their character development will incorporate such
approaches. This will solve many headaches later on and
will help the actors feel more a part of the entire process.

. . . .

Of course the rest is up to you! We have gone through the techniques of drawing nudes and clothing them, adding some Delsarte approaches to figure interpretation. But none of these processes will succeed until you adapt them into your own unique style. This will take hours and hours of practice and application. Start now. Begin to apply some of the ideas into your own techniques. Synthesize. Draw. Read. Research. And keep designing!

In your spare time, study a script of choice and design the characters. Then go back to a show you have already designed and apply some of the Delsarte philosophies as you analyze your work. Why did you choose that shape in that area for that character? Does it make sense now? Could you find a way to enhance the statement?

No process is done until it has been criticized by yourself and by others. The second type will take place all by itself, but the personal analysis is probably the most important. What you learn from this production will make you that much better for the following production. Salvador Dali was asked which of his paintings was his best work. He answered simply "the next."

And so it is. What we do today will improve our work tomorrow. We must keep drawing, keep working, keep researching, and keep studying. Hopefully we chose to design because we want to continually learn. Even as I, myself, finish writing these words and drawing this illustrations, I look back and question if the processes are complete. Isn't there more to discover about the way I can visually communicate with that audience?

My wife has asked me how I can go back and see the same show again and again. I answer, "I'm not watching the show any more. Now I'm watching the audience." I need to know if the visual communication is happening. And the show that does not work is even more fascinating to me than the one that does. I can sit and ponder on the possibilities. How else could I have accomplished the task to make the production a success?

Yes, I know I can blame the acting, the directing, the follow spot or even the audience. But somewhere, deep inside, I still believe I had the power to make it work. And I find myself looking back through the design process, past the fabrics and the makeup and the live production, to the quiet moments at my drawing board when I sat before that blank piece of paper, armed with a simple pencil. Because wasn't that where it all began? And what if I had drawn it just a little differently?

Just think. Think of all the possibilities!